Going Down Gordon Brown

Alice Nunn

Going Down Gordon Brown

with poems by Andrew Mackirdy

With thanks to Sarah Day for her assistance in the editing of the poems.

Going Down Gordon Brown
ISBN 978 1 76041 625 6
Copyright © text Alice Nunn 2018

First published 2018 by
GINNINDERRA PRESS
PO Box 3461 Port Adelaide 5015
www.ginninderrapress.com.au

Contents

Morning	7
Afternoon	46
Evening and Goodnight	71

Morning

This is the day the dots join up. When they have all been carefully connected, I will be able to find my way at last out of the maze. Sometimes I wonder that I could ever have been confused about where the exit lay; every day has made it clearer and through the panic and dismay I still feel a stony relief. All this will pass. Whatever I do and wherever I go, even with time off for good behaviour, I would have come to this point eventually – there are no exemptions.

Nevertheless, the tension in my body is almost overwhelming. If only I could moan and thrash about in bed… But I can't do anything loud or sudden; it's still early. I can only lie here and endure.

This mattress has seen better days and the bed base with its rows of buckled springs is practically antique. My parents slept in this bed at my paternal grandfather's house after their honeymoon – I would have thought it was too small for two but apparently it's a three-quarter size. That means it's okay for people on their honeymoon and who are – I've seen their wartime pictures – still very thin. That was over sixty years ago and I doubt if the mattress has been changed since. My mother has talked about getting a new one and of late has become quite insistent but I've been holding out for a miracle and, if not, there's no need for anything new. So it sags. Like me. Maybe I have seen better days too.

I try to remember better days. Everyone should have better days because if this is as good as it gets, what was the point? What is the point? Joy and life is sucked down the body like water draining, breathing out a sinking feeling, familiar and deadening. I will try to think of better days. Find traceries of gold in the grey fog.

> The lad lay on his back in the green grass
> eyes cloistered against the sun
> listening to the tennis of his parents
> and wondered if he could ever be happier.
> Forty years have since run and rained,
> battered and torn the rents in his personality.
> Never admit to happiness
> for the mice hear these things and with sly
> grins set to their appointed task
> of gnawing the wheel and loading the dice
> so you no longer win
> so you no longer try.

The malign fates are relentless. As each day goes by, their horrible gnawing gets worse. They scuttle about the walls, breathing on my face. I try to divert my thoughts and search for another memory that might qualify.

One bright memory was holidays in Northumberland at my maternal grandparents' house. The smell of damp is nostalgic and always reminds me of that house. Also the sharp smell of tomato plants in the porch, and sweet peas beside the fence. And always the exciting battering sound of the steam trains banging past on their way from London to Edinburgh and from Edinburgh to London. Deep in the night the windows would give a great heave and then the clickerty-clump clickerty-clump rattle until in an instant it had passed.

My grandfather worked on the railways as a signalman and was grumpy with us kids, but one of the people he worked with, Mr Radcliffe, would occasionally let us up into the signal box and there we were allowed to turn the wheel to open and close the level crossing gates and we would hear the dipeddy-dip of a message from down the line and Mr Radcliffe would dipeddy-dip back on the Morse code machine and sometimes – this is a wonderful memory – we were allowed to pull the levers for the signals and there to the south we could see the train coming, blasting dirty steam in great short gasps, and then it was on us, louder than you could possibly imagine and Mr Radcliffe dipeddy-dipping on up the line even as the weight of it was still shaking the signal box. You don't get that at Butlins!

Another memory: I remember coming home after an afternoon sledging, the frost starting to nip at my face as the sun slid down. I sat in the lounge as the fire blazed higher and felt my skin turned to a red glow. After tea and buttered pikelets, I saw in the small gap at the top of the brown velvet curtains that snow was being blown across the black. On TV the funniest man in the world was holding a custard pie and I knew with glee that it would soon be thrown.

But that must be a memory constructed from many traces. When I was young enough to go sledging, we didn't have a TV. In June 1953 (this may be another constructed memory because I was the first to break my Coronation mug), there were only two TVs in the village. One was put in the Memorial Hall for the hoi polloi to watch the Big Ceremony on and the other was owned by the dairyman, and only select persons were invited by for a private viewing. Black-and-white moving pictures on a tiny screen of some toy princess clattering through the rain. It was dull.

Considering we had only just got electricity the year before, I'm not surprised my parents didn't rush out and buy a set, but over the following years everyone in the district, it seemed, was getting one except us. I was twelve or thirteen before my parents got a TV, so I imagine hurtling mindlessly down a slope on a sledge would have been considered a bit childish by then. In any case, around that time they started to build houses along the bottom of our favourite slope. Just where we would normally be sliding to a stop was now someone's fitted kitchen. Change and progress. If only it had all been for the better.

I can't imagine what the shock on my body would be now shushing from hump to hump down an icy slope. Ageing is the most depressing thing of all. The nights are agony. No constructed fairyland of tinkling ice and soft white powder to sink into. Nothing but reality and no redemption. My bones are at screaming point.

> The old man remembered when his body
> was his servant – it did what he told it.
> Now he awoke to something vile and shoddy.
> He tried to stretch to youth as he rolled it
> on his aching side and felt the joints crack,
> wondered whether he could wait for a piss.
> Such indignity, racked by a thousand aches,
> he felt was not meant to be like this,
> not like our parents, we were far more clever
> we were young and would be young forever.
> The divine afflatus gradually retreats
> to a terminal smell under shabby sheets.

But my problem has nothing to do with the minor and ordinary matters of approaching sixty. I have scarcely slept for days. Even if my mattress was comforting and supportive, it would make no difference – all beds are alike to the condemned man. On this, my last night, I have lain awake in this self-made hellhole hour after hour. I have heard the tentative sound of the dawn chorus, followed by an increasingly strident confidence among the birds that the sun will rise. I have heard the stealthy approach and retreat of the electric milk cart. Finally, I have heard the heating system come on, which signals that there is likely to be something passable to listen to on the radio. I can lie here and listen to the news, who's killing and who's being killed, and the state of the stock market. It's nearing the time when I can legitimately get up.

I move onto my feet in dazed compliance like a man in shackles; my execution looms, and I have known for a long time that there is going to be no reprieve.

Something strange has happened to my head. My thoughts have thinned; there is nothing in there for dreams to catch on. How can I describe it? Every time I try to divert myself by thinking of something else, a plot line from a book I've read or a new episode in a daydream where I'm rich and in control, the space behind my eyes refuses to function and throbs painfully. I'm cut off now, cut off from everything even my own imagination. Sometimes I have throwbacks to where the mask smelling of rubber was forced on my face and the fear went up my nose. The only thing now I can do at night is lie and breathe. Sometimes my panic is so great I can't even breathe.

But everything must go on as normal; let there be no suspicion. I open the curtains. My window looks east and dark clouds arch over the newly risen sun – the early sunlight licks at their black bell shapes with the red of guttering ashes. It is going to be another wild and windy April day. I shave myself in front of the mirror over the sink and get dressed looking down into the courtyard which contains a small greenhouse and more plant pots than I have ever managed to count.

The verb 'to potter' was no doubt coined to describe people like my mother spending happy unproductive hours fiddling about in such areas. A few weeks ago during the celebrations for her birthday, my mother left frantic scenes of preparation in the kitchen to go off to do something important. The next thing we knew, there she was out in the greenhouse holding a plant in one hand and a trowel in her other. So much for the important thing she was supposed to be doing. Although who can say what is truly important.

I go down to the bathroom. As I pass my mother's bedroom door, I can hear the radio, so she's awake. In the bathroom, one of the bath taps is dripping, slowly but resolutely. I thought she'd rung him, her fix-it man. He's a retired tradesman who helps pensioners – although he must be a pensioner himself; in fact, he's nearly as old as she is. I always have my heart in my mouth when I see him up a ladder.

As I come out of the bathroom, I notice with concern that there is a light still on in the study. She was in there last night getting ready for today's excursion – she must have left it on and not noticed. She has always been very careful, in fact obsessive, about switching off electrical things – but her sight is deteriorating. It's a small desk lamp made out of the horn of some animal, sitting up the end on a shelf next to the divan. On the divan sits her basket full of china-painting gear. Above, the shelves are full of files, boxes and bulging envelopes full of all the notes she used to use when teaching. She hasn't taught for forty years but she keeps them, in case of the apocalypse presumably. That's the thing about old people: they're the insurance against unimaginable tomorrows – because when the nuclear holocaust comes, they'll emerge from the bunkers with their lesson plans ready to gather up the feral orphaned children and, with gentle patience, start again on the Romans in Britain, the formation of oxbow lakes, the isosceles triangle and how to make jam.

The room smells strongly of oil of cloves, turpentine and earthy powdered paint. I make my way carefully back out – there's a lot of spillage these days and I don't want to get it on my clothes. On the desk is some of the partly finished dinner set she's painting – and has been painting for the last ten years. It's a project which has expanded outwards in inverse relationship to the enthusiasm of relatives to receive it. It now stands at four tureens with lids, eight dinner plates, eight side plates, eight little soup bowls with handles, eight pâté dishes, two serving plates and a lot of square and rectangular knick-knack dishes. Only eight dessert bowls to go. They are a glorious bright red, the heraldic red rose of York set in a design around a monogram with the central letter M.

I've noticed that the older pieces are now a slightly different red to the newer pieces. I think it may be because red is a fugitive colour and the older ones are gradually fading. However, it could also have two other explanations: one is that the formulation of the paint has changed and the other is that my mother's eyes are no longer good enough to discriminate. Is it important that they all be the same?

I go down the passage to the sitting room, past the entrance to the new conservatory. Built with Aunt Winnie's money. Aunt Winnie, the last of the great-aunts. When I was young, there were so many of them, great-aunts and great-uncles, I thought we would never run out, and that there would always be a spare dozen of them around the table at any family function. But one by one we have spent them all until there is nothing and no one left.

In the kitchen, I have to make some decisions. We're running out of everything now. There's enough bread, so I have two slices of toast. I take it easy with the butter but I don't have to bother about economies with the home-made marmalade because Mother thinks it's too sweet and doesn't eat it. There's not much coffee. I'll leave it in case some of her friends drop in mid-morning. I have a teabag instead and listen to the news on the radio.

I hear that Blair is about to rack up ten years as prime minister. And that Hull City now looks certain to avoid relegation. I wonder if either of these pieces of news is important and, if so, which is more important than the other. On the one hand, Blair will get a mention in the history books for surviving so long. That's about it, really: get in and stay there – it's all about endurance, keeping your head above water, outrunning everyone else – then there's an anniversary and everybody claps. Hull City, on the other hand, fights every week, always on the brink, always on the verge of going under, just trying to stay in the second division is one long, exhausting struggle. How can you choose between them, long-term endurance or daily hard-scrabble effort? I must stop thinking about what's important – that way lies sanity.

The weather forecast is exactly what I would expect from looking out the window. I switch off the radio in the kitchen and put on the radio in the sitting room, the classical station, while I play patience on the coffee table; it's what I do every morning, routines on which I hang my life. Of late, I've taken to playing patience and poker on the computer. Sometimes, by concentrating, I can enter a world where everything else is deadened, like being in a perspex booth. Hours can go by until I re-enter reality, dazed and disorientated. But today I need the tactile feel of cards in my hand, as if I know what I'm doing and where I'm going.

The cards are reasonably new and make a soft crisp slap on the coffee table as I put them down. They've been playing Bruch's Scottish Symphony on the radio but then, bloody hell, start playing some ghastly modern piece. There are two forms of music that I dislike. One is the school of assonance as epitomised by Berg and the other is anything that sounds remotely like jazz. Jazz is sheer torture. It amazes me how many people like it and also how many people assume, because you're getting older, that you will like it too. It's as if you get to a certain age and suddenly start liking jazz and wearing braces. A rite of passage, so that on turning fifty everyone is supposed to say, Well, that's the end of rock 'n' roll for me! To hell with The Animals, Janis Joplin and the Pink Floyd collection; enough more than enough of the New Order compilation album; into the bin with the Nirvana Unplugged tape; out with the Red Hot Chili Peppers CD – thank goodness all that's behind me. Now, oh blessed relief, I can start listening to chalk screeching on a blackboard.

> When should you leave a party?
> When Scotsmen start discussing religion
> when Irishmen start singing of their mother
> when Englishmen start praising Maggie
> when Marxists say we should all be brothers
> when the saxophone sounds in tune
> you should leave very soon.

There are young people who like jazz still, I imagine. I think they'd be considered pretty pathetic these days, nerds and weirdos, but when I was a mere lad, there were more of them than you could comfortably fit in a basement flat. But at least nowadays I don't think you could invite an unsuspecting person to a party and make them listen to jazz, I think those days have gone.

The days when I would go to a party at somebody else's place have also long gone. The only parties I've been to in the last twenty or thirty years would be family gatherings for weddings or anniversaries, often not the kind of gathering where music of any sort is played. But even if it were, I would try to be tolerant. Scottish country music, whoop-dee-doo and round we go. Sixties music; it's my party and I'll cry if I want to. My younger sister's taste in music, which is reasonably challenging, I can cope even with that. Yes, even under the extremes of thrash, I will not buckle. Just don't sandpaper my nerves with jazz.

I've switched the radio off and my mother comes through in her dressing gown on her way to the en suite in the downstairs bedroom, where there's a shower. She's pleased with some aspects of the conservatory, the way the sun is lighting it up – this will be its first summer. Aunt Winnie's money took three years to go through probate, and it continues to annoy me that my mother's ability to gain pleasure from it has been curtailed for so long. I harbour dark suspicions about the motives of the lawyers and what was happening to the interest on all the money during that time, but I assume my cousin, who is more worldly wise than I am, would have looked into it. The next most recent money was from great-aunt Sarah and my mother installed the wood heater in the kitchen with that. Each time one of them died, the small pool of nephews and nieces got a share.

Most of my great-aunts and uncles lived to a great age but once they started to die, down they went like a row of dominoes. Funeral after funeral, wake after wake, the crowd thinned so much I no longer had any problem pushing through to the drinks table. Uncle Roly with whisky in hand told me once again about the time he was in Russia when a pack of wolves followed his sleigh through the snow, their eyes gleaming in the darkness like hungry stars, just out of range of his rifle. It's a good story, worth telling again. Uncle Lockhart drank rum. He was a sailor who had shipped troops into every war zone from the Boer War to Suez. He was shipwrecked six times. Four of those times were by torpedo, three in the First World War and one in the Second. When I asked what it was like to be shipwrecked, he said, 'Very cold and wet.' When I asked what it was like to be torpedoed, he said, 'Very loud and wet.' It was a good story too, though short.

The great-aunts were more prosaic, not interested in grandiose history and adventure, more in recipes that required large quantities of best butter. They were women who used to churn their own butter and I've never tasted their second-best butter – I'm fairly sure that such a thing never existed. If it did, it would have borne no resemblance whatsoever to what we buy in the supermarket. I have to remember when I recollect what their butter tasted like that no one had refrigeration in those days and I was eating it at room temperature. I'm sure that if it had been slapped into a rectangular slab, wrapped in greaseproof paper and stuck in the fridge, it would perhaps have been a bit more like supermarket butter, except much thicker and oilier, like clotted cream. What did they think, when they retired from the farm, as they stood in the dairy section of the Co-op or Sainsburys? Did they call it butter as they reached for it? And the bacon in the deli section, when they were no longer able to reach up and slice a piece off their own home-smoked flitch hanging from the ceiling, what did they think of that? Could they see any resemblance. In fact, did they even recognise it as food? But I may be misrepresenting their reaction – it is very possible that after seventy years of grindingly hard work they approached the supermarket with joy; free of all the expectations that comes with home-grown food, they could fill their trolley and sigh with relief that it was all someone else's labour. I will never know. They're all gone, taken their stories and their scones and their sombre mourning suits and departed. As we all must eventually.

The sitting room is a crowded and busy space, full of family reminders. It has some rather delicate mahogany furniture. One such cabinet is stuffed with curios from my grandfather's time in India plus some very nice pieces of Clarice Cliff china, the kind that you see on the *Antiques Roadshow* and go 'Aa-haa!' Mixed in with it is a lot of utter dross of the present-from-Aberystwyth type, objects that someone has paid money for and you wonder why.

The bookcases have had the same books in them for the last fifty years, probably much much longer. Apart from a matching set of Shakespeare bound in red leather that my older sister inexplicably decided to take to Australia with her, I don't think anyone has taken any of the books out since my grandfather died. For a man so reserved and austere, he had a remarkable set of the Romantic poets. Keats and all that sort of swill. Devoid of thought but dripping in feeling, limp young ladies bawling into pots of basil, I can't imagine what he was doing with them. He was a marine engineer and inspector for Lloyd's and perhaps that's the sort of sentimental rubbish they went in for on board ships.

My grandfather lived with us when I was a child. He was a difficult presence, never having mastered any of the domestic arts. Even something as simple as boiling a kettle and pouring hot water into a teapot was beyond him. Back then, people of his generation and class didn't go into retirement homes, they inhabited hotels, and when things got a bit fraught with us, he would take himself off to the Black Swan. I know he had a few pals in the bar and I wonder if he wouldn't have been happier living there full-time, but maybe he too felt that appearances must be kept up and family was family. He came to live with us when I was about two years old so I don't remember the early years but I gather that he very quickly wore out his welcome with my mother when he would leave the table after meals and go and sit in the sitting room and take my father with him. With three children under five, my mother eventually gave my father an ultimatum: if he didn't help, she was leaving. I can't imagine that ever actually happening but even to threaten it in those days showed independence and fortitude. Anyway, either at that time or a bit later when my mother was very ill with a miscarriage, my father became infected by Mrs Beeton and took to cooking with a vengeance, using every pan in the house if he could manage it.

As for Grandpa, he got the runner-up prize, drying the dishes while one of us kids washed. That must have been excruciating for him because he was a fastidious man and our scullery…well, wasn't.

Mother has returned from her shower and gone into the kitchen.

We now have a cleaning lady who comes once a week and she has a go at the kitchen. It was got pretty clean for my mother's ninetieth birthday celebrations six weeks ago and hasn't had time to revert to its old comfortable grot as yet.

I don't mind dirt, I can't see the point of cleaning for cleaning's sake. Why scrub the frying pan if you're going to put in it more stuff to fry straight after? Why scrape the grease off the stove if you're only going to spill grease on it the next day? That is why, although I do everything else, I only do cleaning and vacuuming under duress, such as when someone is coming. My mother does some but her eyes are not that good now. Like all her female relatives, she has acquired late-onset diabetes and for the last three years her sight has become gradually worse. She still drives, slowly and with care. But generally when she goes somewhere further afield, she gets one of her younger friends to take her. It's affecting what she can do but she still managed to complete her butterfly tiles in time to have them installed in the en suite bathroom for her ninetieth birthday. Even now, the latecomers who missed the grand opening get a guided tour. Dozens of British butterflies, painted onto ceramic titles and fired in her own kiln, now flit over the walls of the bath surround.

> In the heat of the cloudless August day,
> the purple buddleia was in full bloom,
> hawking round it a court of butterflies,
> flushed in brightness as they sought room
> on the scented spikes.
> The leaping cat defied gravity
> on its joyful foray
> as it jumped to the height of a man's head
> front legs grasping like a goalkeeper
> to bat the colours down
> to its biting mouth.
> My heart leapt too and cheered
> but I also knew
> the sadness of death
> purple and scarlet lying flat
> and fading on the doorstep mat.

It's time for my daily grocery shopping. I go into the kitchen for the shopping bag.

My mother's eating a boiled egg and watching morning TV. She makes some comment about something she's just seen and then says that we're nearly out of coffee.

I say, 'Rr-ight', my usual response, signalling concurrence with her wishes.

My anorak is hanging on the back of a door in what we refer to as the hall. It's not hanging on any of the eight pegs further down, because there's no room – my mother's coats, jackets and mackintoshes bulge outwards from the wall three to a peg, partly blocking the way through to the garage.

The hall is a large internal space which was constructed when my parents downsized and sold the larger house next door. I can see our old house out of the window, only a few yards away, a roomy Victorian building which had been the replacement for a much older farmhouse. Part of this cottage was the original farmhouse barn, possibly seventeenth century, and converted into living accommodation in the 1920s. It's built from narrow mellow bricks and the door that I take my anorak off is also original, very old and very solid with an enormous key. The hall joins the old cottage to the garage and downstairs bedroom but during the renovations the use of this space, which is as big as a room, was never defined. I've seen those lifestyle programs where people build bigger and bigger houses with more and more unused space in which they celebrate pristine minimalism. How nice for them, to have so much space. And when they get sick of it, they can fill it up with clutter.

Along the far wall is a massive roll-top desk with bookcase. At the other end, a huge glass display case full of china. A small elegant chest of drawers containing hats and gloves sits near the front door. Across from it on the other side is a more substantial piece of mahogany furniture full of tablecloths, napkins and the like. Next to it, a big carved wooden chest holds tennis and other games equipment which haven't been used in years. Three golf bags full of clubs lean against it and the top is covered with bags of library books, and other things in transit. There are windows on both sides and the windowsills are stacked with plant pots and random containers of unidentified bits and pieces.

Behind the ancient door is a ramshackle and more primitive conservatory than our brand-new addition. While the new conservatory is only half full, this one is jam-packed. I remember the old joke that it's time for a new car when the ashtray is full. The builders probably thought of that joke when they came to put in the new conservatory – they offered to pull the old one down. But you can't empty the ashtray if there's nowhere to put the contents. Where did all this stuff come from in the first place? From the psyche of the Depression when no one had enough and when to throw out anything was to leave children starving in China. Old cardboard boxes, fabrics dotted with moth holes, bundles of letters in plastic bags, the personal history you get when you never throw anything away. It used to be all piled on a divan but we had to take the divan out for my sister's friend to sleep on during the ninetieth birthday celebrations and it wouldn't fit back in, on account of all the stuff piled on the floor that came out of the new conservatory and the sitting room so that the twenty guests invited back for drinks after the restaurant lunch would have room to move. The divan has now joined everything else in the hall, gradually squeezing what remaining space there is, constricting passage to the front door.

I go out through the porch into the garden. I've forgotten to bring the milk bottle in; I'll do it when I come back. The sharp air catches in my throat and waves against my face. A blackbird sings from the plum trees round the side, I can't see which one.

> The blackbird stood disabled on the fence
> while her mate looked on from the tree.
> Her stunned pain allowed me to stand up close
> and inspect her leg which stood at half-past three.
> I thought her injury meant she would not last the winter,
> nature is selective and a brute,
> but December I saw them, with him helping her,
> keeping watch while she hunted for food.

In spring I saw her less shabby, some signs of health
the notes turning liquid as she raised her head.
At last I saw them feeding a fledgling with stealthy
alertness. She was getting by quite well.
Kinfolk rallying, a handout here and there,
another cripple makes it through the year.

I like to write poems about the garden. It's walled in brick to above head-height on two sides, with a third side being the house. The road boundary, the only unwalled side, has been planted with trees, leaving the garden feeling safe and surrounded, a place you can barely see. I keep my poems safe too, just a few themes, a few landscapes, a few people. Just words trickling onto the paper and occasionally the solidity of rhyme. It keeps the looming cumulus, the awful outside at bay. Crowded in my room or outside pruning this small plot, I'm surrounded by things I know and can adjust to. But every day, sometimes twice during the day, I walk into town, where nothing can be controlled. It's something I must do.

I clank open the metal gate to run the last gauntlet.

To be nothing requires effort,
everything leaves some trace.
To make sure no one remembers
you must cut bevels on the glass
so they fit exactly and brace
the atmosphere against the pressure of remembrance
so by stintless toil you self-efface
and engineer your disappearance.

I would like to be invisible but I know – I am sure – that I'm not. There's something about being normal that I can't quite get the hang of. Ordinariness is a knack of going with the flow, of looking like other people, of fitting in. I don't think it has anything to do with clothes. My mother buys most of my clothes and I'm sure they're perfectly ordinary but somehow they just don't seem to fit. It's me; I walk too fast and too tensely. If I sauntered slowly along, looking around me with my hands in my pockets, probably no one would give me a second glance, just one of the milling crowd. But I can't do that, it's too painful; every minute as a public spectacle cuts me like a knife. So that's the irony: the more I strive not be seen, the more visible I become.

I usually go to the closest supermarket but today I go to Sainsburys – I know their coffee is cheaper. Also they often have big reductions on food which is nearing its use-by date. I find some chicken pieces reduced to £1.99. I'll make my chicken Guinness pie; I haven't made that for a while. A few potatoes, an economy-size bottle of stout, ground coffee. I'd like to buy peas but they're too expensive. There's a half cabbage reduced, only 99p. I'm in front of the newspaper rack and I buy the *Guardian*, which I do every day. I can't really be bothered with the state of the world any more but she'll notice if I don't buy it. That will still leave me about six pounds if I need petrol…

For a moment, my heart beats frantically in my chest and I can barely get out the money for the cashier.

Walking home, I listen to my breath sawing noisily; I keep my mind blank, try not to look at things. I go through the marketplace. It's grey like an accretion of thick fluff; people move through it like lost socks. I dive down the Garth and back by the beck. This is the full circuit, pretty much the boundaries of my everyday routine. Occasionally I get in the car and go to a supermarket nearby which has reduced prices on certain items.

Sometimes I go even further afield into York when I need to visit a bookshop or to pick up a family member from the railway station or to buy a new suit. I've had to buy a few new suits in the last few years, as I gradually put on weight. I try to rein in my food intake and I suppose for my age and height I'm not that bad but I don't do enough exercise, especially in winter when there's no gardening to be done. There's nothing I can do about that. The days when my uncle used to come and get us all out on marathon walks are long gone.

Walls

At my uncle's we sat out for lunch
in the garden after a hot morning.
As we ate, the clouds started to bunch
and from the grey some drops gave warning.
'John, don't you think it's time to go in?'
'No, no it will soon blow over again.'
The clouds grew black and turned to drizzled rain.
'John, don't you think now is the time to go in?'
'No, no just pull the chairs under the tree.'
The wind sprang up and it grew cold and began
to rain quite hard. We mutinied and ran.
John followed grumbling that he did not see
why a little rain should spoil the pleasures
of the alfresco. I remembered this
at his cremation; the speaker had his measure,
recalling staying out in snow to finish
the picnic looked forward to all week
at his walled-in work. I seek
to understand, walking where once we walked,
notice with worry my now gasping breath,
try to recall of what we had once talked
but all echoes departed with his death.
I eat a sandwich in a whipping gale,
which would have tasted better sat inside
but where I see warmth he saw only jail,
where I see cold he saw spirits untied.

    The small stream running under the bridge is the only intimation of nature in my usual daily round. Although it looks timid and innocent, it can bulge outwards to an angry torrent with startling rapidity. It runs down from the foothill of the wolds and if you walk up the hill to the golf course (note I say *the* hill because that is the only one and it barely deserves that description), then you can see over the whole of the Vale of York, a pleasant vista of smog and cooling towers in every direction.

Where we used to live had a lovely view. We looked out on the Vale of Pickering and there was only one other house in sight. I grew up there on the cusp between the old and the new. The milk was still delivered from a horse and cart, and across the valley the sloping fields were still ploughed by two matched teams of honey-coloured shire horses. Every autumn, we got a week off school to bring in the potato harvest. I can't imagine the current school authorities allowing that. Especially as the lightest work, that of driving the tractor, was done by the youngest. I didn't learn to drive until I was in my late thirties but most of my schoolmates were quite competent drivers by the time they were ten.

We lived about half a mile out of a village on the edge of the North York moors. At the centre of the village on the main road was a dairy farm and the cows would sway along village streets twice a day dropping cow pats. Across the main road was a piggery where the young farmer used to collect his pig turds into a distilled essence which was then loosely housed in a large container on the back of his tractor and he would bounce merrily through the village on the way to which ever field he intended to stink out that day. More often than not, it was the field next to our house. There is nothing remotely romantic about living in the country.

It was an untidy sort of village. They've turned it into a chocolate box since but then the only decent dwellings, with inside toilets and proper drains, were the council houses. The rest were little more than rural slums. Also on the main road was the joinery with its shrieking saws and the dark cobbler's shop next door smelling of ground leather. There was a wooden-shack garage and some dim courts with ramshackle houses.

The butcher used to kill bullocks in his yard. Once with a group of urchins I went to watch the slaughter, a brutal spectacle which probably traumatised me, if anyone understood the meaning of that back in the 50s. Killing took so long – the bullock lay on the cobbled yard panting with its tongue and slowly gathering death. But the sight and memory has never put me off roast beef on Sunday.

The town we live in now is urban. There is an old centre and marketplace but the outskirts are mushrooming developments as it becomes a dormitory suburb for York and Hull. Four-bedroom detached two-storey properties in all directions, most of them with conservatories. These developments have brought wealth to the town; it has reinvigorated the area and there is yet another major supermarket chain about to set up shop here.

The arrangement with my mother is that I pay for the groceries out of my pension – I get £81 a week – and my mother pays for the heating out of her pension. I think she gets a bit more than me, though I've never asked. Those two expenses more or less swallow up both pensions. She pays for the other household expenses such as rates from her other sources of income, shares and so on. We do all right, I think. I mean, we're not going backwards. We don't eat like kings but we don't starve either. Lunch is our main meal, as my mother doesn't like to have a heavy meal too late.

The gate is open when I get back and the milk bottle has been brought in. I can hear animated chatting from the sitting room.

'Hello,' I call out as I go through into the kitchen.

I put on the kettle while I'm putting the provisions away. I automatically switch the radio on; they have yet another talkback program with people lauding the new drive to kick bludging pensioners off their payments. I switch it off again. That's me, a bludger. I have been one for more than thirty-five years, ever since my early twenties. I live quietly not drawing attention to myself and have tried to help where I could. I do the food shopping, I cook the meals, I do the washing and hang out the clothes, I prune and dig the garden, I do vacuuming under direction. I allow my mother to be a free spirit, doing the things that she has always done. Fine embroidery, lead lighting, china painting, pottery.

If people put more value on her work, I would be seen as a hero and not as a villainous sponger. Last year, she put some of her embroidery in an exhibition in York and sat there demonstrating pulled thread work while the public came through. The organisers were worried they wouldn't get enough patronage to pay for the hall but in the end thousands came, thousands and thousands, and academics buzzed like bees around a honeypot. You don't get one of her pieces off a machine; they take weeks or months, sometimes years, of concentrated work. You don't learn that at a few evening classes either; there's a lifetime of tradition passed down through great-grandmothers, grandmothers, great-aunts and mothers and sisters. And the public are all gazing on thinking, how does she do that? All those three-dimensional swags and leaves. She was rather chuffed that the academics were interested and taking photos of her work. But why should she let them take photographs for free? If they want it, let them pay a premium price for it like they would a painting or a sculpture. That design was her great-grandmother's. You can't take a design from an Australian Aborigine because they have copyright in their work. But elderly women are easy to steal from.

Anyway, my point is this: my mother is living out her old age comfortably in her own home at no expense to anyone and I should get credit, not brickbats and the hangman's noose.

I pour boiling water into the coffee plunger and find three matching cups and saucers out of the cupboard. I find the matching sugar basin but I can't find the milk jug from the set. It's in the dishwasher, where she put it after breakfast. I wash it and fill it with milk. My mother likes things to match. Also, these are what she calls the 'best' cups; there's a division between these and the everyday cups but, due to concentrating on her butterfly tiles, my mother hasn't painted many cups of late and in any case the cups that end up in the cupboard tend to be the seconds that she can't give away as presents. Those used for best are nevertheless better than the everyday cups which have lost their colour or are chipped and in every other household would already have been thrown out.

There is one thing, though, about having so many cups and saucers: it means no gathering, however great, could ever exhaust our ability to provide tea and coffee. If Jesus on the Mount had decided instead of loaves and fishes that everyone should get a cup of tea, I hope he would have turned to us – we can provide. And if it's a cup of tea and a biscuit, that's no problem either, because my mother goes to umpteen charity afternoon teas and comes back with umpteen packets of home-made biscuits which she herself is not supposed to be eating. Yes, if we could just exist on tea and biscuits, we could slide through to the last trump, no problems at all.

I take the tray into the sitting room, push the plunger down and pour out cups of coffee while responding in my usual way to the exclamations and questions of my mother's friends. Once the social niceties have been adequately dispensed with, I return to the kitchen to start the initial preparation for lunch.

I pour myself a large glass of stout. It's cheap home-brand stuff and I doubt there's much alcohol in it. I start putting the ingredients together but suddenly realise with horror that I'm missing some. I feel a welling up of panic, incapacitating, immobilising. I do what I often do when beset by terror: I switch on the radio. The talkback is over and they're playing Tina Turner's 'Only the Best'. I immediately start to revive. My sister said that she got drunk at Christmas lunch some years ago and sat in front of a Tina Turner video with a Berocca until she came right again. When she went back to join the others, she found someone had drunk her Grange. Apparently drinking someone else's glass of Grange in Australia is a hanging offence but due to the power of Tina she was able to grandly forgive. Now she says she turns to Tina for many other of life's ills and has always found her to be efficacious. Of course, a woman that age strutting around the stage in death-defying stiletto heels has to put everything else in perspective.

I'll find substitutes for the things I'm missing, I will not panic. I breathe in time with the music, I gulp some beer. Maybe I should have lashed out on a cheap bottle of wine. No, let's keep it together.

Song
Do I take the last glass?
For the first
the nose and taste were great
and with little sips
the next three were convivial
but I now rotate
the bottle about the sediment.
Shall I take the last glass?
It will take me over the eight
knowing the pain to come
but I have paid for this whole feeling
of elation – this happy buzzing
which is close to bliss – and so
I drain it to its dregs.
Alcohol tears the carapace
breaking shells and weeping over
the place where shields don't grow.

Chorus
When we kissed you were so large
my arms were thrown out wide,
urges that in dreams had charged
were surging up to hug my side
with girls tanned and buttocks lean
bodies thin as magazines
now chasms of limbs outstretching
opening things once secret
breaking shields and fetching
a season for regret.

    The pastry is made and resting in the fridge. The chicken is cut up and marinating in the stout. I'll put it in the oven at twelve o'clock. My mother comes in carrying the coffee things, her friends having departed. Fortunately, I've already put my glass in the dishwasher. She thinks everybody's got an alcohol problem if they drink more than one glass. I'm sure both my sisters drink as much as me, if not more, but the difference is they drink in social settings and I drink alone in my room. I'd quite like to be an alcoholic but I can't afford it.

I go up to my room until it's time to put the pie on. It welcomes me in. I've lived in this space for many years and it's very small. Small though it is, it doesn't constrict me – quite the opposite. I'm comfortable here on the shores of tranquillity. It contains my possessions, nearly all of which I can do without. When I come in here and shut the door, it's as close as I can come to freedom.

There are 842 science fiction paperbacks floor-to-ceiling two deep on shelves beside the bed. I prefer to read science-fiction because I know nothing embarrassing will happen. Everyone is either good or evil or a mad scientist; I like the ordered two-dimensionality of the genre. Nobody smells or makes weird noises or says anything inappropriate in space. There's no clutter in their sitting rooms. You don't have to examine anyone's feelings for half the book. And most people and places have peculiar names which make them not quite real, as if they're at a distance and knowing about them can't harm you. Any nasty messy human interactions between characters with strange names is as alien as…

Question. What's brown and sticky and comes from planet Zog?

Answer. A stick.

Warning: don't let the sticks implant themselves in the soil because once they put down roots… I once wrote something like that for my school magazine. It began, if I remember, 'By the light of a burning shoe shop, I noticed the first tendrils sprouting from my ankles.' One of my humorous masterpieces.

Another of my school magazine masterpieces was called 'A Page from a Detective Novel'. I still have that magazine.

> The room had been ransacked. Herlock Sholmes saw it at once. 'They're on to me,' he thought and threw them off. He went over to the desk and poured himself a stiff slug of Coca-Cola and soda. Just then he heard a sound behind him, so he dived to one side, drawing and firing his .303 machine gun as he fell. He was only just in time; half an hour later a shot rang out. 'Drop the

gun, mister,' said a voice. He did, and accidentally dropped it on his toes. After he had finished dancing around the room, he was frisked, but they didn't find his .33 bore shotgun or his .45 automatic in their sheaths strapped to his legs. 'Thank goodness,' he thought. Just then they found his .33 bore shot gun and his .45 automatic in their sheaths strapped to his legs. 'Oh, well, while there's life there's hope, I suppose,' he thought. And just then they shot him.

It wasn't very good but it amused my classmates. And I like a good detective novel, though I don't buy them because I can get them from the local library – they have a good selection. That's a trip I do once a week, to the library, but funnily enough I feel quite comfortable when I get there – it has an old-fashioned feel to it although it's in a modern building. I pick up books for my mother too. She likes her detective novels a bit more Gothic than me. A picture on the cover of a house with one lighted window, a sinister cast-iron gate, vaguely creepy undergrowth, is a fair indication that it's her sort of book.

As well as all my sci-fi books, there are also two shelves of poetry books which I cherish with some care, unlike my other books, which I look on as merely artefacts. All the greats are there, the ones who I admire, the likes of Emily Dickinson, Philip Larkin, John Betjeman, Carol Ann Duffy, Tony Harrison, Roger McGough. *The Oxford Book of Sonnets*. I do like a good sonnet. I like any form which can compress the human condition into a very few lines. Emily Dickinson did it best; she probably had the same short attention span that I do.

> My words lie here flat on the page –
> I treasure these cripples.
> When it echoed round my brain
> this was a large and noble poem –
> now it's on the page small and bitter.
> Maybe if you shout it you will hear,
> what should have been.

My room is L-shaped, with my bed and bookshelves under the roof away from the window. Against the end of the bed is a chest of drawers. It contains my shirts and underwear and winter woollens, many of which are too small or in tatters. There's a bright blue shirt, the colour of morning sky, that my sister bought for me more than thirty years ago. It's as neatly folded as it came out of the packet, unworn. On top of the chest of drawers are many more books, some with circles of wine on the cover. There's a wardrobe against the wall with my suits in it, most of which I can't get into any more. The two most recent ones are hanging in dry-cleaning bags on the back of the door. The beige one I bought for my sister's wedding three years ago and also wore to my mother's ninetieth birthday celebrations last month. I've expelled colour as far as possible from the things I wear, shrinking inwards to neutral shades.

There's a television sitting on my chest of drawers but it doesn't work. I don't know why; it hasn't worked for some months. I told my mother and she said I should take it down the road to get it fixed but I don't know how much that would cost. In the end, it doesn't matter. I only used it to watch sport, which I can't do on the one in the sitting room because soccer and cricket irritate my mother. She likes tennis, the Olympic Games, that sort of thing. Most of my contact with the world has never been through television anyway; it's been through radio. I listen to the radio all the time because, unlike TV, you rarely get sprung by anything upsetting on radio. So it's the background to my life. I know all about films I've never been to, artworks I've never seen, books I'll never read. My sister went to the British Pavilion at the Venice Biennale and the moment I saw her photographs I knew who the artist was, what the controversies were, what his artworks sold for at auction. Between the radio, the *Guardian*, and the Sunday papers, you can become ridiculously well informed. Politics, science, international affairs, I don't think there's any subject I couldn't talk intelligently on if the opportunity arose. Of course it doesn't arise because I don't go anywhere or see anyone. I chitchat to my mother's friends and from time to time members of the family arrive. My sister in Australia only comes about every three years because of the distance and expense, although she has been coming more often of late. My brother from America comes over more regularly, probably once a year. My younger sister from Sheffield comes over quite often but the intelligence she brings from her world is not something I can contribute to.

This sister is considerably younger than I am. As I was growing up, my mother had a number of miscarriages which left her in bed for weeks at a time. We would be given the glad tidings by my father that the expected brother or sister was not coming after all. Then one day there were strange women in the house and strange messes in basins and my father told me with great jollity that I was no longer the youngest and told my elder sister that she needn't think she was the only girl any more either. My younger sister's advent was therefore a source of great anxiety to all of us. The age difference, though, was too great to make much difference to us older siblings. She was born into a different decade, and it felt sometimes as if she was born into a different world altogether.

My father was rather puritanical in a jocular way. His wartime letters to my mother contained critical descriptions of other women who wore make-up or strange hairstyles or inappropriate clothing – he affected to be shocked when he found out that she was also a 'slave to Yardley'. But he needn't have worried; lipstick and powder were the extent of my mother's toilette. I wonder how it was for him producing someone like my younger sister. She went to art school and made extraordinary fabrics, wore odd combinations of clothes and bizarre hairstyles and sparkly eyeshadow. She came home for Christmas one year wearing a black referee's outfit, pink tights, pantomime dame boots and a plastic elephant dangling from one ear.

She spent her time after art school forming bands, breaking up with bands and occasionally playing in bands. Once, my father asked her why didn't she give it away and get a proper job and I remember her anguished cry, 'But I'm talented!' We all have our talents, big and small, but most of us are just pissing in the wind.

She got married three years ago to a man who also plays in bands and is interested in the music scene. Together they own more records than you can reasonably fit in a three-bedroom house. For her wedding, she wore a lime-green sparkly dress with a bouffant skirt, a 30s-style fascinator and green glitter stilettos. She carried a bouquet of orange flowers. Her husband wore a lime-green shirt. After the reception, still in amazing array, she lugged the remains of the wedding cake through the centre of Sheffield to the massed astonishment of its citizenry. That's the kind of life she leads. It's a world where everything is vaguely amazing. She talks about the kind of people and events which are never broadcast on Radio Three.

Apart from my siblings, however, visitors are now getting thin on the ground. In a past populated by umpteen million elderly relatives, I can remember when there was a fairly high turnover in the spare room, but those days have gone; they're all dead. I'm turning into somebody elderly myself. I grow old, I grow old. I make light of it: what pate through yonder hair shines. But it does worry me. I've put on weight. My hair is grey and I'm going bald. One day I woke up, looked in the mirror and my grandfather was looking back. Maybe I expected nothing to change, that I would be a lanky dark-haired boy forever.

> The real rips out the hull
> and kills the floating dreams,
> catching sight of greying hair and dull
> blotched skin, a youth no more it seems.
> The mind must have lost its place
> to see cragged wrinkles on a teenage face.

I sit down in my chair, which is old and beat up, one of the cast-offs from downstairs. I take my notebook in my hands but I won't open it now, too late. I've been transcribing my poems into this book but as I write them I must tinker with them and so it all gets no further forward.

> It started well
> full of passion and surprise
> all body's lusts and brain's ideas,
> but then the tropes began to cool
> and thoughts became more hidden as the meter
> began to bind and rhyme schemes caught
> the errant metaphor and made it peter
> out into the last couplet
> which instead of wild cheering
> was as flat as white bread.

No point railing at failure. It happens to everyone anyway. Everyone approaching sixty is going to think to themselves, oh shit, where did my life go? Once, I had great dreams, of being a scientist, a famous poet, playing cricket for England, winning the Nobel Prize, saving civilisation. Now I wish I had just got rich. That is the gathering insecurity of getting old.

My mother will die soon. If not this year or next year, then in a few more years. And I'll be alone. The prospect is just as frightening as everything else. The house is left to all four of us siblings but it can't be sold while I live in it. The problem is, I won't be able to afford to live here. We barely get by at the moment with two pensions. I couldn't afford both food and the cost of heating this house and the council rates are the same as the big house next door that we used to live in. Apparently this cottage has got character and the Victorian four-bedroom, two-bathroom, three-living-room pile next door hasn't. In an ideal world, I should get the house, after having lived here and looked after my mother for so many years. But this is a world where such an inheritance would affect my pension, making it even more difficult to maintain an existence here. Well, I don't have to worry about that any more; everything has a silver lining.

I pick up the science-fiction novel that I've half read but I can't concentrate. What's the point of reading a book you're not going to finish? It's just reading for reading sake. Also, I have to say that I'm not that bothered what happens in the end. If I read science-fiction because it doesn't impinge on the real world, then by the same token the denouements, which are usually fairly bleak, very rarely convince me that they could actually happen. Which is good in a way because I don't enjoy reality; my own imagination has always been enough to frighten and depress me. I don't need anybody to do that for me in a book or a film or on television. That's why I like the radio; it's like a walled garden where you can sip on gentle fruit while somebody explains Kropotkin.

I take up one of my many notebooks again. They're all curling and distressed and my poems, my cripples, loiter furtively within. I've written my feelings about them: how the words strain across paper which must endure the degradation of a failed attempt; what they try to be is mute but what they are is drivel. So what are they for? Maybe to please a paupered spirit. Poetry is the sepsis oozing from an infected wound, I write, and all poets are damaged. All biographies describe hairy insects trapped in amber and if the subject is completely covered in neurosis, it cannot decay. I write these things – and they're true for me.

This one is an old school exercise book, from boarding school. I went first to the local primary school, just down the lane from where we lived. It was a two-room stone building which had served the village since Victorian times but was suddenly, overwhelmingly, too small. The infants' class had to be housed down in the Memorial Hall and the Education Department was scrambling to build a new school near the playing fields. The post-war baby boom had arrived.

It was an old-fashioned school. In the morning, we all chanted Good-morn-ing-Miss-Wyatt-Good-morn-ing-Missis-Wilson. Then it was times tables by rote, three-eights-are-twenty-four, four-eights-are-thirty-two. Then writing practice, my favourite time for ink blots with pen nibs dipped in ink wells and transferred (some of it) to exercise books. Best of all were nature walks with Miss Wyatt, when we would plunge into deep meadows intent on naming everything we saw.

Mid-morning, we would have our milk and play marbles or conkers or rounders in the small concrete playground. At noon, we would snake down through the fields to the Memorial Hall for a two-course hot lunch, a gift from the authorities, along with free cod liver oil and orange concentrate, as part of their post-war fears of malnutrition and rickets.

School was just part of everyday, barely separate from life on the land. Everything I ever knew about British wild flowers, trees and nature I learnt at this school, and the older boys from outlying farms discovered they could suck up to Miss Wyatt by bringing in rare woodland plants and hedgerow flowers with their old country names.

But the world was changing. Children were having to stay longer at school and a new secondary modern opened half a mile away. If you failed the 11-plus, you were sent there to rot quietly for four years before being tipped out on to the scrapheap. I wasn't expected to pass the 11-plus. That's why I went to boarding school. A more expensive route for arriving at the same fate.

It's time to put the pie on. I go down into the kitchen and shut the door – this is my domain now. I like to have the meal on the table at exactly one o'clock. I put on the radio again; it's a comedy show.

Now here is an interesting question. A man awaiting execution is asked if he has any last requests. He says yes, he would like a comedian to visit, and names the funniest man in England. So this comic turns up, sits down in the prison booth opposite the condemned man and starts his routine into the microphone. The comic does this absolutely brilliant half-hour and the question now is, does the man awaiting execution laugh?

And here is the answer. Yes. A sound is surprised out of my mouth like breath departing; I hear it with astonishment. It was like when I sat beside my cat as it was dying and I heard it purr. How could that be? Surely there should be an absolute solemnity at such times. Apparently not. Somebody should write a comedy set in a respite ward for the terminally ill. There's a lot of funny stuff happens in such places, my Australian sister told me; she used to work with a palliative care doctor who kept them in stitches.

Apparently, here's a little known fact: all of this doctor's patients stopped dying during the Sydney Olympics. My first reaction was, it's Australia, they're all sports mad over there. But I don't think it is that, I think it's the communal nature of the event. They don't die just before Christmas Day either, though they can depart in shoals on Boxing Day. They want the event of Christmas, and the mind can control the body, even in extremis. They want Christmas even though they know they'll get shit presents. What do you buy a dying man for Christmas? Something shoddy that will wear out quickly? Or something quality in the giver's size? Or something from the supermarket marked 'use immediately'. Boom boom. Little jokes, little explosions of breath.

> Another Christmas over and once again
> Father Christmas never came.
> I have been waiting for that bearded pain
> for 40 years and have an archive
> of burnt bits of paper put up the flue
> to flag my needs and all I ever got
> was an orange in the stocking toe
> and tinny little toys that broke,
> never the Ferrari or a buxom strumpet
> or the ability to play the trumpet.

The pie is ready to put in; I just need the oven to be hot enough. I go into the sitting room and start to read the paper, hunched over it as if I really care what goes on in the world. Something moves at the window, a bird probably, but for a minute I think it's Tammy. She always jumped up to the middle one, looking in in that vaguely startled way as if someone had unspeakably insulted her for no reason by keeping the window shut. She would sit there indignantly, demanding entry.

> Goodness shines from your eyes, innocence catching the light,
> you simply deny any deviation from the right.
> Though unworthy I must speak up and ask how come
> there's a dead bird on the doormat. And don't try playing dumb.

Another death in the long cavalcade. Another one under the

ground, whispering memories into winter branches. The long march from the lip of the glacier, from the pure, melted snow, down into the sodden muddy valleys. The wind moans. The paper tells me we're a bankrupt country governed by gutless men, that companies are run by thieves, that a beggar lies face down in the street and no one stops to see if he is alive or dead. The poor are vulnerable to buzzwords and the media hack their stories from those who can't fight back. I see myself, and those like me, trampled bleeding in the mud in the name of economic rationalism by a party that was supposed to support us. And the awful thing is, I die for them because I have no choice; there is no one else to help me. I put the paper down. The window is empty.

> I cover her eyes from the soil
> with my old grey jumper.
> She would not have liked the way
> her mouth hung open so inelegantly.
> One last stroke of her velvet head
> then pile earth over this last betrayal.
> Lay the snow pure on the black shore,
> cover over the small absence,
> chill the air of all life and freeze the soil to stone,
> another small enjoyment is gone.

Life is a series of small things. I never had any grand adventures; I don't even know what that would feel like, whether I would have liked them if I'd had them. Like the shipwrecks that Uncle Lockhart found all too much of a good thing – he was much more interested in talking about his garden: how the carrots were coming on, which roses were in bloom, small everyday things. 'The Boy standing on the Burning Deck' makes a popular poem but most people would rather read about it than do it. By contrast, people don't want to read about ordinary life, about cleaning out the kitchen drawers. Even though I'm sure there's riveting stuff kept in kitchen drawers. It's my guess, for instance, that most people keep their kitchen scissors in the second drawer down. My kitchen scissors, as a sign of individuality, are hung on a hook on the wall. This is a fact which is not even slightly interesting to most people but if I read it in a book about someone else, I would feel the faintest flash of recognition. But anyway this is my life, prosaic and rooted in objects, small habits and timetables.

Time to prepare the vegetables. I peel the last of the potatoes and wonder what to do with the cabbage. Boiled cabbage on its own doesn't appeal. I wonder what Tina would do. There's an apple which has seen better days and I add it. When it's boiled, I'll add the last of the butter and a pinch of nutmeg. Only the best, better than all the rest. On the radio, there's a talk show of some description. One of the speakers says that any healthy relationship with a vegetable is a quasi-religious act. Despite Tina's encouragement, I can't imagine having a relationship with a cabbage.

> I once had an affair with a carrot
> but we split up over differing views on the Trinity.
> Although the cauliflower and I both agreed
> on the bread becoming real flesh in the sacrament,
> our relationship was otherwise unhealthy
> and led to some unusual
> cauliflower cheese.

It's nearly one o'clock and I start to clear a space on the table in the other room. This is another of life's daily tasks: clearing spaces that have become covered, moving piles of stuff from one place to another place, where they then get lost; negotiating an ocean of clutter into which things sink.

Three years ago, my mother bought some new tights to wear to my sister's wedding but when the day came for her to leave for the ceremony, enormous effort was expended without success in trying to find them. After the wedding, my Australian sister was going down to Cornwall, taking my mother's mobile phone so she could ring me to pick her up when she got back into York. She asked where the charger was and after about an hour of searching, the box was found, I forget where I found it but when I opened the box, I produced, like a rabbit out of the hat, my mother's missing tights.

I don't mind it myself, because I have very few things to lose. The newspaper and the pack of cards are my entire contribution to the sitting and dining area and I move the newspapers into the kitchen next to the stove on a regular basis. But of course most of the clutter in the kitchen is mine – food, bottles of this and that – but I can usually find most of it if no one else interferes.

> My visiting sister is very precise
> which is all very nice but a bit of a bugger,
> she puts the rice in the jar marked rice
> now we've no place left for the sugar.

I go in search of my mother, who is sitting in the conservatory holding a book, with her eyes closed. The sun is streaming in and it's quite warm.

'Good book is it, Mother?'

She blinks her eyes open and says, 'Oh.'

'Dinner time,' I say and go back into the kitchen to dish up.

When she eventually comes through, I'm seated at the table with the pie in front of me and the vegetables in two separate dishes. I've poured myself another glass of stout and put a small glass, for form's sake, in front of my mother's place. She won't drink much of course.

'Oooh,' she says, 'have you made your pie? What a treat.'

I feel a twinge of guilt. She never questions what I cook and of late the menu hasn't been that flash. Most of the scrimping, however, takes place at teatime, when I can get away with soup or something made with leftovers. Still, it's good that… I shut down that thought quickly and serve her a piece of pie. I let her help herself to the vegetables while I take a good big sip of stout. The pie is delicious. It's a recipe I often use but this time it's better than ever; all the little substitutes seem to have worked. What a pity that…

'I'm supposed to eat kale,' she says. 'Cabbage is good too but not as much. I forget what for. The eyes, I think. Oh, this is very nice.' She eats appreciatively. 'Lovely, thank you, Andrew.'

I bob in my chair, a sit-down version of a bow. 'Would you like some stout?' indicating the bottle.

'Just a very little.'

I pour her a splash. She makes a good meal and I have two helpings. No point being frugal now. I drink the rest of the stout, I feel replete, rich and meaty.

I have over a dozen dishes like this – pies, hot pots, lasagne, curries – which I usually work my way through in the course of a month. Tuesday we always have fish and chips because that's market day and I can get fresh fish off the fish stall. Sunday we always have a roast; I prefer beef because Yorkshire pudding is one of my specialities. Monday is usually cold meat with vegetables or a salad. The days plod along in a predictable way with no surprises.

When my younger sister comes with her husband, I have to cook something vegetarian for him. When my Australian sister comes, she always wants pork pies. It's apparently something the Australians aren't very good at – perhaps there aren't any Olympic medals for it. Apart from that, our neighbour across the road occasionally gives us a trout he has caught. That is my *pièce de resistance*, stuffed trout with almonds. It was my father's recipe and the secret, the ingredient which no one will admit to these days, is suet. I use a lot of suet. I make my pastry with suet. Not butter, not first-pressed olive oil, nothing low-cholesterol or heart friendly. No, a nob of unredeemed animal fat. That's my secret. Possibly it's other people's secret too, I'd be pretty sure that the pork pie has got a suet pastry and that's why it doesn't taste the same in Australia. From what I can gather about that country, they spend all their time running about in the sun with zinc-creamed lips, drinking vast quantities of beer and chilled gooseberry-dry white wine and following the fashion fad for a low-fat diet that recreates the hard tack of their convict past. Well, good luck to them, if that's their thing. I intend to go to the grave eating nice pastry.

I put the cake on a plate that my mother brought from the Women's Institute last night. There's something about events organised by or for women that always seems to involve cake. I've often contemplated this and the reasons for it. Perhaps it's the maintenance of harmonies by sugary treats. It doesn't seem to extend to men.

My father was fond of one of his own anecdotes. He went to London to meet with a financier who had been helping one of his clients and the man offered to take him out to lunch – somewhere, boasted the financier, with 'home cooking'.

'Oh,' said my father. 'Stew.'

This always got a laugh. However, if he had said, 'Oh, cake,' there would have been a completely different dynamic to the statement.

There can be good or bad stew but there can only ever be bought or home-made cake. I have a fine appreciation of home-made cakes, I was brought up on them. My mother's chocolate shorty lives in the realm of legend, her ruff-puff pastry slice with home-made jam and cream was another favourite, and every December she was up in the wee small hours of the night nursing the Christmas cake through to perfection. The cake, which I have just taken out of its wrapping, is a tea cake iced with pink icing and little silver bobbles. Tea cakes, in my view, are one of the hard ones to get right – along with scones, they're not for the beginner. I'd say without tasting it that this is one from the upper end of the echelon, plenty of heft and not too dry. I make a pot of tea.

Mother is going out this afternoon and is already fussing about, trying to find things. She thinks her glasses are in the red handbag. I eventually extract the red bag from under the computer but no glasses. After a while, they're located in the other red handbag under her sewing table. She wants to take one of her slumped glass bowls and she thinks it's down in the cellar. This is serious. I go out of the kitchen into a narrow space which we use as a laundry and pantry; it runs under the stairs and in that space is a lifetime of mending. I think there would be at least fifty sheets with holes sitting there waiting for the day when my mother turns them outside in. They've been sitting there for at least twenty years. Personally, I don't want a sheet with a seam down the middle of it – my bed is lumpy enough as it is. However, I'd never be game enough to suggest that we got rid of them all. Thrift is a terrible disease. It saps at space, filling every corner with things that may come in handy. It slowly strangles you with objects. It keeps alive the barely remembered anxieties of the Depression which would be much much better buried and forgotten.

I have to move everything so that I can open the trapdoor. This is no doubt one of the reasons why this cottage has character. Unbeknownst to the council, there is also a well under the kitchen floor which as soon as it was discovered was quickly covered over before they could find out about it. But the cellar accumulates so much moisture that there's barely any need for a well. My elder brother on one of his trips from America bought a dehumidifier and after I've rather cautiously negotiated the damp stone steps, I go over to check it. It's full to overflowing.

The cellar is the size of a room and because of its dampness only hard rubbish can be dumped here. It has an ancient multi-pane window and, looking out, the ground is at eye level. There's something strange and unnerving about that. Birds sometimes stand a nose length away pecking for worms or on frosty mornings turning over with resigned acceptance a slurry of fallen berries.

> The cotoneaster weighed down with berries, untouched by birds
> until a hard frost. Then they are all feeding merrily,
> and fighting any newcomers crossed in the maul.
> It must be rice pudding to them.
> A dubious treat mostly, but on a cold day
> a nice change to a hungry longing for meat.

There's a table covered with various bits of ugly silver, tarnishing quietly. When who-gets-what comes up, I always say that I want the silver. However, my mother says, 'But you'll just sell them all.' True. Some of them are family heirlooms, which doesn't make them any prettier. I feel sorry for my older cousin, who's going to have to find house room for them when my mother dies.

There's a cardboard box full of my mother's 'glass phase' on one of the benches. The cardboard is wet to the touch. I carefully take out the bowl she's wanting.

I go back up to the living room. Every step I take, every action I perform, is resonant with the significance of it being the last time I'll walk here, the last time I'll perform this simple action, such as pouring tea for my mother, passing the cup, cutting her cake which she is not supposed to eat.

The living room is full of the colour and busyness of my mother's pastimes. The sun shines in on the painted china plates crowding round the picture rail, lighting up the lead-light partitions and lampshades she has made, glinting on a slew of subterranean needles buried in the carpet around her embroidery frame. The home is a dangerous place, full of chemicals, high-temperature ovens, sharp objects under foot. A lot of people die at home from domestic accidents or because they just want to stop breathing. But there's the other danger that we might not die but keep on living uselessly day after day, moving from one room to the other, engaged in small and insignificant actions, trapped on a treadmill of habit.

My mother's nearly ready now, coming in and out, saying this and that. I sit near the window reading the paper pretending to engage but tight as a bowstring waiting for her to go. She has no idea. I know what devastation I'll leave but there's nothing else I can do and now it seems right, the obvious thing.

At last she's ready. She goes to the loo one more time 'just in case' as she waits to be collected. The doorbell rings, there are exclamations and chat, then she calls goodbye and goes.

I listen while the car departs. I'll leave it quarter of an hour in case she forgets something and has to come back – an unlikely event but it has happened. I sit upright and unmoving while the clock hand slowly moves through the motions. My brain is empty like a vast echoing cave, no small things, no mundane actions now to hang on to. Tick tick tick pound pound pound like troops marching, the horizon is a cavalcade of advancing menace. The execution corps is bringing its tumbrel and soon I'll be jolted down the road towards the heaving blade.

The thumping stops. I get up, take the car keys from the hook near the front door, and leave.

Afternoon

I back the car out of the garage then get out and pull the door back down. I wouldn't normally do that unless I was going for the day. Of course, I am going for the day but I don't want to send that message. I don't want to send any message. Mainly I don't want to think about Mother coming home later this evening.

Because I have done this before.

17 September 1971: father to sister

We were glad to have your letter, and if your proposed date of departure is correct, this will be the last letter from home to you in Turkey.

Andrew seems to have been accepted by the Civil Service, but is waiting his call-up, as it were. He doesn't know when or where he is going. Mary-Lou is now a third-former and entitled to wear a skirt.

David rang up the other evening. He had just enlisted at the Evening Institute. What subject? I gave the family a twenty-question session and after about fifty suggestions had to tell them: judo. In the furious silence, Andrew said that David probably didn't like sand being kicked in his face.

6 November 1971: great-aunt to sister

When I was in Harrogate, your parents had lunch with me. It was very nice hearing all the family news and the parents looked happy and well. I'm glad Andrew has a job that may prove interesting. If he is at all 'polite-calling' minded, dealing with health and education might be stimulating, or was it health and housing? Anyway, interesting.

7 November 1971: father to sister

Letters 1 and 2 from the kibbutz have now arrived. We are hoping to see David in a few days' time. One major item which has knocked us sideways: Andrew has disappeared. He simply went off, not even taking a toothbrush. And not even leaving a note. The first few days involved panic, but this has now partly subsided. He is operating his chequebook from Earls Court. Part of the background is fact, but most of it is conjecture. The fact is that he was successful in applying to the Civil Service for an executive job. The next stage was that he was notified that he would be appointed to the Department of Health and Social Security, based in the London area, and would be notified of the actual office to which he would be attached, in due course. The Soc Sec people also wanted some unimportant details about his insurance cards. The following day, he buzzed off. My conjecture is that he is demoralised after months of hanging about home and that some irregularity in his cards had, in his mind, reached gigantic proportions. So he quietly took the train to London instead of the bus to Scarborough, where everything could have been sorted out. We didn't know about the insurance card trouble until after his disappearance. I am hoping that a letter I have written to him, care of a bank where he cashed a cheque, will reach him. All I know (and from this we have some sense of relief) is that there is no need to worry about the police, the hospitals or the mortuary. I will let you have any further news as and when it reaches me. Mother will be writing. Weather cold and stormy.

> Hit an oil drum
> sounds vibrate in emptiness
> ask me questions
> receive the same echoes
> tell me why I sit
> and am alone with no future
> how to pull myself from this mess
> except in the vacuous dark
> an idea grows.
> Razored arteries
> will absolve me pure.

25 November 1971: father to sister

This will be a morose sort of letter, though things could be a lot worse.

The lad came home exactly a week ago. I had the ghastly job of breaking into the bathroom on my return home at teatime (Mother hadn't returned from her weekly outing to York). The poor boy was unconscious from loss of blood; but he recovered consciousness that evening in hospital. I went in, ambulance chasing, and they patched him up and gave him a couple of bottles of plasma, and physically he is now all right. Mother stayed home with Mary-Lou, who wept bitterly, but she is all right now too.

Tomorrow Rose and I are going to York to see the psychiatrist. No doubt there will be a scientific name for it, but I think he simply reached a state of despair. He had been wandering around aimlessly, and had slept rough before making up his bewildered mind to come home and end his days in relative comfort. He is now in Naburn Hospital, York, and I believe will be there for some weeks. He is quite sane, if you don't boggle at the word, but very subdued.

Rose and I have got over the initial horror and a handful of people have been very helpful, so far as they can be. My monkish friends have been saying their prayers with us in mind. I expect this sounds pathetic but it helps. Mary, our neighbour, at the height of the crisis was a good standby, and we also took into confidence the local rector whose wife is professor of sociology at York, and seemed knowledgeable and very helpful about this kind of situation.

We have wished you were, I mean had been, at home; I think you and Andrew were much closer together than Andrew and anyone else. David is coming through this weekend from Bristol.

There isn't any other news that seems of any importance.

We are looking forward to your next letter and hope to learn of your plans, if any. There is no need to contemplate rushing home. I have no reason to doubt that after he has had the usual treatment for depression, or whatever, Andrew will recover his spirits.

The turkey has been ordered for Christmas, if you'd care to join us.

The weather has been appalling, with great snow drifts. Mother can now add a few choice lines.

25 November 1971: mother to sister

We both send fond birthday wishes. We shall be thinking of you.

I saw Andrew in hospital this afternoon and he is brighter. I took in a case of clothes and he will be able to walk about now he has them. Physically, he seems to have gained strength and is showing an interest in reading again.

David's firm is on strike again so maybe he won't be able to come. He is contemplating buying a car.

7 December 1971: father to sister

We have greatly appreciated all your letters. Mother, who is learning to type, might even get around to typing out the series dealing with your trip to Jerusalem.

We are now seeing Andrew, together or separately, twice or thrice each week. He is still being tested and no particular treatment is being given. But he is having to attend recreation, involving playing table tennis or cards with another human being, and I don't think he likes it.

David came through ten days ago at the weekend and the contact was a good one. He gave Andrew an autographed biography of Freddie Trueman.. Mother sees Andrew on Thursdays and we both saw him this weekend. He has his moments of humour but is now, I fear, guilt ridden on top of everything else. He winces at certain points and we therefore glide over anything to do with his past and keep to the inane or innocuous subjects like his appetite and his socks. Has considerable intelligence, the doctor said, but has lost the power to use it.

> It was just the result of choices made
> early by indifference
> not driven by evil or the devil
> instead all that was built was a wall
> to cut me off and so

there was not even enjoyment in the fall.
Lord, the gift you gave is returned unused,
I never did grow into it

7 December 1971: father to sister

Andrew, I fear, is trying to shut out the past. In doing so, he is also shutting out parental love, such as it is. I wish we could do more to help. I feel like a non-swimmer watching a kid that has got out of his depth.

Your letter dealing with the trouble was helpful and both of us nodded agreement. We both remarked on the similarity with a very kind letter from a not very old Ampleforth monk touching on what he called his living death. (In the first panic, I thought Andrew might have shut himself away from all contact with us, and wrote to the youngish monk, who had met Andrew, asking him if he could supply a familiar face at the hospital, if need be. But in fact, our relationship with Andrew has hardly been dented.)

The dining room is being decorated.

7 December 1971: mother to sister

I am spending a lot of time visiting Andrew. He is quite chatty and can see the funny side of things but he is now beginning to hate being there because of the odd people he meets. Sometimes I feel quite cheerful when I leave and sometimes depressed myself. I'm driving myself to do more work than necessary. We have half the spring cleaning done!

12 December 1971: mother to sister

We are making this a Christmas letter. We had two letters from you this week, for which many thanks. It does help us to have letters from you and it is comforting to have help from both you and David. Your deeply thought-out letter was a help. Some of it I'd thought out or been aware of for some time but hadn't the wit to seek medical help.

It was a little chip no larger than a fly,
a crack no wider than a pencil line,
gradually wandering in small strikes
that eventually ran together into the black night
sundering under internal pressure.

It had had too much weight put on it.
The cracks started gently at the top
then gradually spread
and the purling china ticked
as the filigree parted
along the lines of weakness.

The potter cut the diamond from the biscuit
and did not smooth the cut enough,
propagating lines of fracture
which are now quietly divorcing
to release the stresses from the faults of firing.

12 December 1971: mother to sister

We visited Andrew yesterday and he has shown some improvement each time. On Thursday when I went after lunch, he was fast asleep in an armchair. I think he is given sedation tablets. However, he now shows an interest in news items from home and village. Great-aunts Margaret and Elsie have sent some sort of get-well card which he treated with wry amusement.

I hope you go to Bethlehem at Christmas and finish your intended stay in Israel. There is not much you could do if you were here beyond visiting and this is something of a strain. I see a time ahead when you might be able to help. David suggests (although this was when he was missing) that he would get a bigger flat and Andrew could stay with him and proceed from there. I'm not sure if that would be a good idea either. At first we wondered if Andrew had turned against us. Although I don't think this is so, it may be wiser that he doesn't come home here when he is better. We flounder about in our thinking hoping that we'll do what is best for him but now being so unsure.

We are now going to try and make Christmas as pleasant as we can for Mary-Lou. I don't know if Granddad will join us or not.

17 December 1971: great-aunt to sister

I'm so sorry Andrew is going through such a sad experience. He had too much time to think and read. That sounds grim but these days one must have concentration on a job of work to make some sort of balance in this disturbed period of time.

20 December 1971: mother to sister

I am enclosing a cheque which I hope you can spend. I'm trying to get it (the letter) written against Mary-Lou's chatter and the great subject is that one of her friends has had some Christmas presents stolen. Also the tray she brought in for a quick cup of tea has just over-balanced. David is now at home. Granddad wrote saying he wouldn't come this time. It was suggested that if we apply we could get Andrew home for Christmas Day. Daddy has written to the doctor about this, so whether she allows it I don't know. David can now drive so he's going to trot into York on his own and visit Andrew. He is improving and now he is having electrical treatment. The first one gave him a headache but he told us on Saturday that the next one hadn't affected him at all.

> The eye turn red and the skin burns
> in anticipation.
> The room shrinks and turns
> in a low slow spin of spit.
> The skin knows its fate
> and begins a sluggish shiver
> but the mind, a bit late on the uptake,
> tries to make some sense
> of the searing taste in the mouth.
> The brain belatedly starts fearing
> its end has come and knows
> that it has not done
> its duty.
> Punishment weighs by the ton.

> The burning line along the lashes
> the flashing burn upon the lids
> the evidence has been heard
> and the jury is returning,
> let me receive mercy and not justice.

6 January 1972: father to sister

Needless to say, we have all been dining out as a result of your Christmas greetings from Bethlehem... Andrew has finished his electrical course of treatment. He seems quite relaxed (most of the time) and is talking of leaving hospital. Hitherto, this seemed a matter of indifference to him. Not that he is ready for a discharge yet, but I think is gradually throwing off that fatalistic nothingness... Andrew wasn't allowed home for Christmas, and we were discouraged by the nursing staff from paying him a visit. I expect this is a mixture of running the place on a skeleton staff, plus an emphasis on the community (if not the Christmas) spirit.

16 January 1972: mother to sister

Andrew is home again. I had written to his doctor to say in effect that he was back to 'normal' (Andrew's normal) and the depression appeared to be cured even if a personality problem remained. He is glad to be home. The next stage is an appointment with a careers advisory officer who will, no doubt, be supplied with the hospital's assessment of the psyche, or however they care to put it. Meanwhile, life proceeds as usual but with Andrew not volunteering for any task which might bring him into contact with friends, neighbours, villagers, etc.

Did we tell you that we have developed a dishwasher?

> We were unprotected
> in the rush
> to end our final session.
> Our separate ills were cross infected,
> I got thrush
> and you got clinical depression.

My sister came back from Europe in the summer of '72 having ignored the barely concealed hints in the letters that she return earlier. I have no doubt she did that out of self-preservation. Families are hell.

No, that's not right. Families are fabulous up to the brink of adulthood. But there is a tipping point and then everyone should scarper and head for the hills. If you stay home after that, you'll be forced to either write Gothic romances about t'moors or to kill yourself. And those who do take themselves off can't be responsible for or feel guilty about those who don't.

My sister worked in Scotland for a couple of months and then left for Australia, where she's living still. My brother went to America not long after and then my cousin (my father's niece) settled in New Zealand. My father's family had lived all over the world, so this was not a surprise.

On one of my sister's return visits a few years ago, she went to a reunion at her old school and remarked with astonishment that many of her classmates were still living in the same neighbourhood where they grew up. She couldn't understand it; she thought that as soon as you could, you got as far away as possible. She thought those were the rules. When you came from an area which her headmaster referred to in his broad Yorkshire accent as a 'cultyeral wilderness', breaking the apron strings was not done with dainty scissors but with a meat cleaver. Separation has to be effected brutally and forever.

A rush for the exits, but I never quite made it. Some months later, I had another go but the police brought me back.

> I moved back to my native place.
> I count myself a failure.
> To be successful is to be anywhere but here.
> This will not pass.

> A year of pain
> when everyone who touched me cut
> into me with a blade. The world
> was a box of glass.

So I stayed home with my parents. I did start a novel, but it was more noir than Gothic. Like so many things, I never finished it.

Only my younger sister seemed to have no need to escape. Once, when she was eight or nine, she apologised for turning up late at her best friend's house in the village by saying she had been messing about with her oils and had forgotten the time. Her friend had a tame magpie which went round with them, sitting on her friend's head. They didn't live in my world so why would they need an exit when they were already somewhere else? Absorbed in her art, in making things on an old knitting machine she found in the cupboard, in turning ugly lumps of clay into other ugly lumps of clay, my younger sister seemed barely aware of the enervating lassitude within our structured routines. And of course there was a big change. We gave up the house in the country and moved here, to a small town not far from Hull. Supermarkets; shops; a cinema; even – a late development – a nightclub.

Did I really buzz off because of some letter from a bureaucrat? It's so long ago I can't remember. More likely it was because my first experience of work was so mind-numbing and dispiriting. Who on earth in their right mind would think I was a good fit for an insurance office? But there I was in 1971, receiving a call-up again for a war that I could never win, to join again the workaday battalions on the battlefields of life out there beyond any possibility of control. It was a letter that destroyed comfort and order, and look, I've received another one. This one too has reached gigantic proportions. History goes on repeating itself. The power of the pen, only nowadays it's a computer. The power of the faceless bureaucrat and I could have been one of those, someone in Social Security who destroyed other people's lives all in a day's work and went home to fish fingers.

Anyway, the upshot of my first break for freedom was that I was diagnosed with post-adolescent schizophrenia. Possibly this was right at the time; I don't want to judge the state of my mind back then. There was a voice inside my head saying, 'What's the point, what's the point?' over and over. Everything was emotionally muted and it was hard to concentrate. All I know is, I wanted to be far away. I went down to London like a moth to the light and busted my wings against hard railway bridges and unwelcoming doorways. When I was forced back, it was to a dark cave where life was barely lived and I crept inside and rolled the stone across behind me.

Whether it was the right diagnosis or not, there was a certain satisfaction all round that an explanation had been found. I was put on a pension and my father joined the Schizophrenia Foundation and eventually became a member of the board. He seemed to find this activity soothing, as if he was doing something useful. Somewhere down the track, I decided that I didn't have schizophrenia but had clinical depression. But I didn't tell anyone; it seemed better to just keep plodding along in the old way without any upsets. I didn't want any more doctors. Even for the normal ills of life, this oppressing breathlessness I sometimes feel, I avoid doctors at all levels.

So, as I was saying, here I am again, without a toothbrush, breaking out. I shut the gate and get back in the car and drive out of our small neighbourly court. There's no one around, which is good; no one to see me go.

I'm soon out of the town into a flat farmland patrolled by tractors, fields heaving under the plough. The trees are not yet in full leaf and have a ballerina-green impermanence, skittishly twirling around the edges of a landscape uniformly brown like endless chocolate soup. In the pale sky, a glider hangs like a foraging raptor. This is the place for riding the updrafts. Over to the left, against the escarpment on the edge of the wolds, above the sharp fall of land where wheat fields meet sheep, I have seen brightly-coloured young people hang in the harnesses of their hang-gliders on long summer afternoons, rising and falling and creaking like huge arthritic birds. But now a cold wind still scours with the sounds of a saw's screech which would freeze the unprotected like grapes left for ice wine. Ne'er cast a clout, and May here in a couple of days.

> May is the cruellest month
> when suicides reach their peak.
> The stamina that takes me through
> the cold, hoping that the bleak
> days are what brings the misery,
> ends when sun and blooming blossoms
> brings knowledge to a head
> that the sterility is me.
> Gardeners say to leave frost-burned shrubs
> at least another month to see if shoots
> come from the base
> but I know when the roots
> are scorched and the core is dead.

I'm heading towards the coast. Everything's going well, so I'll turn my thoughts to death. Death makes ephemeral outings when you're young. Old relatives die just offstage and birds rescued from the cat expire overnight in shoe boxes. People from the village, who you used to see, simply disappear and there's a certain amount of shuffling and coughing.

I only vaguely remember Uncle Ronnie dying. He was my aunt's first husband and my mother wept while hanging out the washing. My grandfather came out to tell her to pull herself together. I was impressed by that. Clearly, weeping was not something we did in our family, even under provocation.

Was that memory before or after I nearly died of the measles? I don't really remember the time. I may have been younger or I might just have been too sick to remember. The doctor had been called and had prepared my parents for the worst, that I might not make it through the night. I wasn't loaded into an ambulance with sirens and flashing lights to travel the hour or so to the nearest hospital because, I suspect, modern medicine at that time had no antidote.

Anyway, I survived and lived to adulthood. But once there, I found that the older you get, the more people who die. It gets personal. People who you have known all your life depart and holes appear, those mice again gnawing at your foundations, turning the life you knew into something else. I understand why people in other cultures rip their clothes, tear their hair and wail. Death peels your history off the wall. It leaves you naked in a world that doesn't care about you.

> My aunt lay willing herself to die.
> I tried to think of something to reassure her -
> that I remembered her at her peak -
> but the husk that lay there forbade me to lie
> and at that extremity
> what truths could I speak?

I forget what sort of cancer that aunt had. My father got cancer of the breast. Twenty-five years ago. There was a lot of toing and froing to hospital. That was when I plucked up courage and learnt to drive, out of necessity. There was a lull, and everything went back to normal. My father returned to work in his practice as a solicitor.

For some time previously, I had been helping out by going in a couple of days a week to do some bookwork for his building society agency. He had left a successful well-established partnership to come to this town, eventually setting up in practice again in his late fifties completely from scratch. His new practice was busy but not particularly lucrative. The one part of it which did pay was the commission from the building society work, which grew steadily. He told me once in the early '80s that he had been negotiating with the society to pay me a full-time wage of £60 a week. He asked me whether, if this eventuated, I could put up with my mother's cooking. I replied that if they paid me £60 a week I would eat at the pub.

As well as bookwork, I used to assist with deceased estates where there were no immediate family members at hand. I enjoyed deceased estates. First of all, you would go in looking for documentary evidence of their lives. Where they banked, whether they had shares, what they owed – all their written history. For most people, that comprised no more than a scanty line of figures, eighty years of life reduced to one page of a bank book.

I wasn't so much involved in that as in sorting out the artefacts. I see those archaeology programs where prehistoric princesses are dug up wearing their wealth of brooches and bracelets. Surrounded by the common plots of people who had nothing. Most of the deceased estates that I helped with were of the latter variety.

But in today's prosperous times, even those who have nothing still have a lot of possessions. No one has just one saucepan even if they live alone. No one has just one of anything. Even the most rabidly monastic has at least two chairs and several cups. These possessions tell their own story, piecing together a life that has been lived. These will be our grave goods and from them future archaeologists will hypothesise on our lives and deaths.

Sometimes, the story is of a person who has just outlived everyone, which sometimes happens with very old people. Sometimes, the story is of bad luck or bad decisions, pathetic clues from a futile existence.

> The market stall watch only cost two pounds
> and kept good time until the power drained.
> I threw it in the bin as that I've found
> is cheaper than having the battery changed.
> The office clerk made sure he kept good time
> diligently attending so he could
> secure his place and this would let him climb
> to middle management and acquire good
> pension rights, dreaming small dreams not knowing
> his firm thought him just a pair of hands
> and found it worthwhile to keep him going
> only till he was slowed down by the sands
> of time. Then he found out with bitter shock
> his life had not been worth a carriage clock.

It is best not to be judgemental about what you find in other people's houses. We all hide things in our sock drawer that we should have thrown out years ago. So I would rifle through a lifetime's accumulation and sort out the stuff for the auction rooms, bag up stuff for the charity shops and offload the rest at the municipal rubbish dump. Maybe I should've gone into that as a business. So many people die there must be a quid in it.

Nearly five years after he was first diagnosed with cancer, my father went to the hospital for his usual check-ups. The doctors told my mother he had six months to live. They didn't tell him, however. My mother went up to the post office and wrote letters to everyone so he wouldn't see what she was doing. Every time I go in there, I can see the grief etched into the writing counter.

He had nearly died forty-five years before in Normandy, which, in a vague sort of way, I knew about as I was growing up because his legs were so scarred. But after his first diagnosis, he seemed to be catching at his past and he resurrected a description of his wartime experiences that he'd written in 1948.

I'm not sure where he was, I don't think he knew himself, except that they were trying to break out of the Normandy bridgehead. His platoon was advancing into action and he was shouting out to his men to watch out for tripwires. Almost immediately, he himself caught a tripwire in the long rough grass. He was blown up in the air. His sergeant and batman couldn't find his field dressing because most of his trousers had gone and the field dressing pocket had gone too. His wristwatch was shattered but still ticking (without its glass and hands). He remembered these details. All he said to his sergeant was 'Well, I am a cunt.' Yes, my father said that word. Who would have thought it? I've never said it aloud in my life. But war is not a time for polite conversation.

But it wasn't the explosive device that nearly killed him. It was a British tank. The stretcher bearers took him to a German dugout being used as a signaller's post. He lay on his stretcher on a bunk waiting for an ambulance. The sun streamed in through the entrance. Hours went by. The signal officer offered him cigarettes and so on, but in an embarrassed helpless sort of way. The noise of war continued and no ambulance turned up. He looked at the timbered ceiling of the dugout and started to groan. How comforting, oh, what a relief it is to groan, he said. I know how he felt.

There was a sudden cry from the entrance to the dugout – a tank was coming straight at them and everyone dashed out, leaving him there. He heard the tank grinding on to the dugout. He watched the timbered roof; the timbers squeaked and sank; the whole ceiling was coming down on top of him! And then, it didn't. It must have sunk at least a foot – but he blessed the German field engineers because the tank rolled on and the roof of the dugout stayed put. He said he didn't know it was possible to be so frightened. I can imagine what it was like for him, in a place of safety, at the point he realised that it could also be his tomb. Lying there helpless as his own side lumbered over him, oblivious and en route to some greater goal.

And now there was another ceiling coming down on him. Eventually he had to be told that it had spread to his lungs and there was no treatment. He gradually wasted away.

> Heels thrown up behind him as he ran
> to catch the bus, the half mile
> down to round the bend.

> 'Run Daddy run!'

> The village could set their clocks
> by his pounding shoes.
> Now his feet prop forward from the loo
> trying all the while
> for dignity with a sheepish smile,
> the stertorous breathing at the blocks
> and a three-yard sprint for the finishing
> line of the bed.
> He lies back spent
> the pillows plumped around his head.

> 'Stay Daddy stay.'

The house filled up with grief, affecting everyone except my father, who was on steroids and bursting to communicate in a positive way with people he hadn't written to for years. He decided he wanted to die at home and oxygen bottles appeared along with other medical paraphernalia, home nursing service personnel coming and going.

The days slid by in quiet pain like we all had muffled rocks in our chests. Six months exactly, almost to the day.

> It was 9.30 and another nervous day unwound,
> I had come down to make the supper
> when I suddenly heard a whimpering sound.
> She came in and said, 'Andrew he's gone,
> he's gone. I thought he was sleeping
> but he's gone.'
> She put her head against the kitchen door.
> I put my arms out to her weeping.
> There was nothing I could say.
> She said, 'I'd been lying down beside him
> glad that he was sleeping.
> Then I went to get the tray.
> When I came back he was gone.'
> In her tone there was a sense of betrayal,
> that after forty-seven years he had somehow sneaked away.

He left no instructions for a funeral. He had for years been very interested in the Christian faith and had been part of an ecumenical group. He had once gone to a religious conference in Spain with a parson and a Roman Catholic monk. They had monastery-hopped down through France and had had the religious equivalent of a wild time. But in later years he tired of organised religion when his deafness meant he could no longer follow the service properly. He said he didn't care where he was buried. In the end my mother decided on a tenth-century church not far from where we used to live in the country.

Tears? What tears? Me, cry! I never weep.
In the grey Saxon church my eyes began to seep
water as King James and John's many mansions
undid me by their ancient scansions.
There is no place that is not broken.
Fallen are the walls and lions
come from the caves to reclaim their stone.
If, for my father, the words unchoke
the unteared truth fossilized in bone,
then the old yew trees beside the brook,
with silent pools where the current runs,
bend arms to shield the sundial from the sun.
Time is ended. In shadows look, the light has gone.

We all selfishly dread orphanhood. We can never replicate the level of unconditional love that a parent bears for a child; every other relationship is less wholehearted, less forever and more based on inclination. So the burden of loss is very heavy when one parent dies. When both parents die, we lose all the love we have always accepted as our right. How very alone I will be then. I always believed the journey should continue, however, while my mother still lived. After that, my thoughts and expectations were totally blank.

Time goes by but it doesn't heal. When you live a small constrained life, the loss seems to grow greater rather than less. Never a day went by after my father's death without that loneliness breaking in, that vacancy where he used to sit, that silence where before there was long-nosed laughing at my jokes. I missed his kitchen mayhem, the atomic bomb that seemed to have gone off whenever he was let loose. I treasured his cavalier recipes.

His recipe for the Sunday roast was:

Take any typical Sunday and a 4-pound piece of brisket. Get up and switch the oven on setting the regulator at about 450°F. Cook the breakfast while the oven is heating up. Just before eating your breakfast, put the brisket, fatty side up, into a large roasting tin and bung it into the oven. Don't worry about dripping – the brisket will do the worrying while you are having breakfast.

After breakfast, look inside the oven. If the brisket looks browned off, take it out of the oven. Put about 2 cups of water in the roasting tin, and then put a lid on it. Reduce the regulator to about 320°. Shove the whole lot back into the oven and peel the potatoes. Spend the rest of the morning washing the car, digging the garden, reading the *News of the World* or going to church.

40 minutes before dinner, put the potatoes on to boil. After 10 minutes, take the potatoes off the boil and the meat out of the oven. Pour the potato water down the sink, and the liquid from the roast into a metal jug or basin. Turn the heat up to about 420°F. Put the potatoes round the brisket, and splatter them with some of the fat from the top of the liquid in the metal jug. Leave the lid off this time when you put the brisket and the potatoes back into the oven.

Cool the metal jug as fast as you know how. When the fat has solidified, use the stock underneath to make gravy the way granny used to do; alternatively use Bisto. Turn the potatoes over, and when they are properly browned, dinner is ready.

The clashing of his knife sharpener and his carving knife signalled the fact that lunch was on the table and he would push his glasses down his nose, saying, 'Let the dog see the rabbit,'

A few years ago, my sister wrote from Australia and asked for my recipe for Yorkshire pudding. I found myself writing it out as if he were dictating it.

Andrew's Patent Method for making Yorkshire pudding

Take four tablespoons of strong flour. Add 1 egg and a pinch of salt. Gradually stir with a spoon, making sure to crush all of the mixture with the back of a spoon against the side of the bowl. Gradually add milk to keep the mixture a stiff paste. (To stop yourself stirring too quick, try singing something slow and ponderous like the national anthem.) Leave to stand as a stiff paste while the joint cooks. About 40 minutes before the meal, take some meat juices and fat from the joint and put into a baking tin and heat the tin until the fat sizzles. Dilute the flour mixture with milk to a thin paste and add to the tin and then cook in the hottest part of the oven, about 250°C.

We used to eat it cut up into squares with the meat, but the proper Yorkshire way was to eat it as an entrée saturated with gravy. Ah, gravy. Not stuff out of a packet. Why anyone would want to pour coloured flour and water over perfectly good food I don't know. No, I'm talking about real gravy.

If this had been planned, that would have been my final meal. Not the chicken pie, which was surprisingly nice, but when you're going out of this world, you want to taste the very best of the pleasures it has to offer before you go. No, on second thoughts, my final meal would probably have been steak and chips. I would have got out the old chip pan for the final time, stirred the ageing fat in it and put it on the stove to heat to boiling. Then I would have cut the potatoes into big chips, none of these thin straw things which seem to be fashionable. When it was fizzing with heat, I would have put in the chips and let them fry until they were crisp and brown. I would have put my mother's steak on first, because she doesn't like any colour in it at all – if it's even slightly rare, she thinks she'll get food poisoning. It's one of her set positions, like going round and switching everything off at the plug every night in case they catch fire (a habit which gave our new television set a nervous breakdown).

What would we have with the steak? Oh, salad, I think, as it's nearly summer. Tomatoes sliced into oil, vinegar and chives. Shredded carrot with preserved ginger. And crisp lettuce leaves with a light dressing. A really nice wine, rounded and smooth. One of my mother's summer puddings to follow with thick cream. And then coffee and some of the chocolates she has left over from her birthday.

There was no planning to all of this. I was caught by surprise. I went last Monday to get some money from the bank and it came up 'Insufficient Funds'. I felt the breath drain out of me. Of course I knew it would come sooner or later but had turned my eyes away as if, by not knowing, I could somehow put off the inevitable.

There was no planning in terms of the time. The longer the better, but eventually your time runs out. But this bit has been planned, I have known for weeks that this route would be the final journey.

I come to a roundabout and nearly go the wrong way. I'm not familiar now with the country. One road goes south to Humberside airport. I went there a few weeks ago, taking my sister to catch a plane to Paris. That was when I got the idea. That road goes over the Humber Bridge and there's a dizzying prospect of space beneath. Many people have jumped from the bridge. One young man jumped recently, an affair of the heart. He rang his jilting girlfriend and, with his phone camera on, recorded live for her his plunge through hissing vindictive air into eternity. He made it into the paper, through a coroner's finding – a species of fame, because most suicides are never reported, in case people want to copy them. I wouldn't want to copy the phone exploit. I want something much more private but that leap, that steep stack of space, was in my mind as we drove over the bridge that day.

We had been talking about Hull and its new developments and I said any one however thick could see the potential and if only I'd had the money... My sister pointed out that to borrow the amount of money needed I would have to have had a job. I laughed. Yes, what was I talking about. I had chosen another way, or it had chosen me. My journey didn't come with my own car park, my own office, the keys to the beer fridge, a thirteenth-floor balcony to plunge off in comfort any time I felt like it. My road came with little in the way of material comfort and what little there was got less and less.

> Walk with me the serial killer
> who keeps on murdering self for spite
> grains of malice from the miller
> thrash the chaff away from light
> when the unused self is strangled
> but flowers again its staff to sound
> rip it from the rope that dangled
> strip it off the stone that ground
> knead it to the soil unneeded
> bake unleavened an unlived life
> salt it with the tears unheeded
> cut it with a water knife

again each day the mind reprises
changing deaths each day unlived
halt the bloom the yeast surprises
in the dross of life unspared.

Another road is to Hull. My father's parents moved there when he was young, and it was where he was brought up and went to school. He met my mother before the war, when she was teaching there. Until quite recently, the scars of war rippled still through the centre of the city, flexing among dreariness and rubble. The Blitz had been constant.

My mother said that one day after many weeks without respite from the bombing, the powers-that-be decided that the school where she was teaching would leave Hull forthwith and several buses appeared to take the children to the country. No one knew where they were going, so it was an adventure for one and all. The buses drove for about an hour and then stopped. They disgorged their passengers into a field and drove away.

I've been looking around wondering if any of the fields I can see were that particular field. They all look pleasant enough from a car window. Green and lush, in summer they would be purple with clover, a sprinkling of dog daisies, herb willow near the hedges. On a fine day with the sun warming you, I expect it would be very pleasant to throw yourself into the grass and listen to the thrushes singing in the hedge rows. For ten or fifteen minutes.

My mother and her pupils were left there all day with nothing except the sandwiches they had brought with them. There was no shelter, no desks, no chairs, no blackboards, no chalk, no books, no toilets, no water, nothing. These were city kids who had no knowledge of, and no interest in, the country. It was the longest day of my mother's life. And something broke in that field. Before that time, my mother had assumed that the people in charge were competent and well chosen and knew what was best. What a frightening revelation for a young woman away from home for the first time (having left a tiny village and entered a sea of mayhem, of dropping bombs and burning buildings) to realise in addition that the war was being run by morons. If Churchill wondered why he got voted out at the end of the war, I can tell him. Too many people ended up in fields.

Anyway, it didn't happen a second time. I can imagine all the children going home and telling their mothers what they did that day. 'Yer what?' Whatever nincompoop thought it up seemed to have forgotten that children have mothers. Mothers of young children are dangerous people to cross.

> The bantam cock trapped me and my sister in a corner
> darted towards us with glory in our fear.
> Mother heard our screams, came out with her broom
> and broke its neck.
> We ate it roasted with chipolatas.
> Don't mess with me, Sunshine,
> or I'll set my mother on.

Despite the Blitz, Hull during the war seemed to have been a surprisingly jolly place. There was a large army encampment nearby and even though the skyline was burning, everyone still went dancing. Pretty young women had swarms of admirers and several of these swains laid their hearts at my mother's feet. She had a powder-blue two-piece evening gown, very un-Hull in my view; I just can't visualise any sort of elegance coming out of that place. I always associate the city with dock grime and the close-ribbed scruffy streets of Philip Larkin. Awful jazz records played endlessly.

> When assonance turns to dissonance
> bile drowns the rhythm of the dance
> and the flat waste years pavane their steps,
> and the little that was fair
> slides down the noisome grate.
> The ears and acid stomach turn
> to malady forcing feet to stick
> in mid figure of the reeling set.
> I hoped for a last clear trumpet

the sound of an honest note
but I am going down to a jazz saxophone.

I have to go all the way round a roundabout until I can get familiarised and I eventually manage to exit on the correct road. I don't know this area very well and I'm now quite tense, not wanting anything else to go wrong. The closer I get to my goal, the more fraught is the project. However did I get to this point? It doesn't bear thinking about.

Many years ago, I saw a program on Henry VIII and his six wives, it was a drama on TV and one of the wives tells Henry VIII a joke. I don't know whether it was a real mediaeval joke or made up by the scriptwriters. Anyway, a man is condemned to death by the king. He says to the king, 'If you'll put off executing me for a year, I'll teach your horse to talk.' The king is intrigued and agrees. But the man's friends ask why he proposed such a foolish thing as he's only putting off the pain to another day. The man says, 'A lot of things can happen in a year. The king might die. The horse might die. I might die. Or the horse might talk.'

Since my first sentence of execution over thirty-five years ago, I have been trying to teach the horse to talk. But even with all my efforts and all my scribbling, even if the horse could talk, what possible things of interest would it have to say? Horses have nothing in their heads of any importance. So a talking horse, once its freakishness was acknowledged, would just get the usual rejection letters: move along, nothing to be seen here. Yes, the man's friends were right, why put off the evil day hoping for a miracle. What has to be done just gets harder and harder.

I'm on the coast road now and I can see the sea pounding out towards the horizon. Everything whirls and heaves and my blood pumps. I'm getting closer and closer and I can now think of the task ahead with a higher excitement, the upper reaches of fear. I must close my mind to everything else and concentrate.

I am the master of this ship
forcing whitely against the waves
wind gusting on my mouth and throat
pushing hard against all delays.
I hear the beat of rising breakers
and point the helm towards the land
crash through the ebbing undertow
and smash the hull onto the strand.

    I turn into the car park, find a spot and switch off the engine. This is the end of the line.

Evening and Goodnight

The letter arrived in its cheap brown envelope from the pension people. I shouldn't have been surprised. I had already read the headlines in the *Guardian* that Gordon Brown the Chancellor of the Exchequer intended to remove at least a million of the undeserving poor from a cushy comfortable life on the pension. I knew also that this is always a possibility when the economy is strong and the sudden increase in the unemployed figures is not likely to raise unease in the electorate. By that, I mean their electorate, Labour party seats. It's very popular to get those with a bit of a bad back out of the pub and back into gainful unemployment. But I had sunk so deep into the system, been lost for so many years that I barely noticed the coming and going of brown envelopes.

> I lived contented in the Arctic waste,
> listening to the frozen bells,
> gazing at hexate crystals cased
> in the glistening windows of my cell.
> I ventured nothing and gained the same -
> a zero sum which kept me sane

I never thought that the changes would apply to me. About ten years ago, a new manager had come to the local branch of Social Services and had discovered my name on the list of pensioners living in his area. He prised me out after a visit and brought me in for an interview. I heard nothing further. Obviously he found me sufficiently odd to satisfy himself that I was not worth bothering about. I therefore assumed that I would move gracefully from my current pension on to an age pension in the course of time and keep on doing what I was doing until my mother died. I had never thought any further into the future than that.

On 6 September 2006, the letter said,

WE NEED SOME MORE INFORMATION

We have sent you form IB50 with this letter. Please fill in this form so that we can see how your illness or disability affects your ability to work. Read the questions carefully. It will help us if you answer the questions as fully as possible. If we need more information we may have to ask you to attend a medical examination at a later date. You do not need to get any supporting medical evidence from your doctor.

Quite blithe in tone. Nothing really to be scared about unless you weigh up the subtext. I filled it in, all the questions. It was difficult. Which box should I tick? The hardest thing for me is trying to appear normal and this is always what I aim for, so I must constantly guess what the right answer to each question is. I'm not good at guessing what normal feels like. In the end, I ticked the boxes even though most of the questions were quite strange.

'Was mental stress a factor in making you stop work?'

I ticked Yes. That's fairly uncontentious. The civil service were hardly going to offer me a job after my breakdown as they have enough loonies working there already.

'Do you frequently feel scared or panicky for no obvious reason?'

I ticked No. I always know the reason why I'm scared or panicky.

'Do you avoid carrying out routine activities as you are convinced they will prove too tiring or stressful?'

I ticked No. I'm looking after my mother, so I have to carry them out whether I like it or not. Who else is going to do them?

'Are you able to cope with changes in daily routine?'

I ticked No. Disruptions are stressful.

'Do you frequently find there are so many things to do, that you give up because of fatigue, apathy or disinterest?'

I ticked No. As above, I don't have the option of giving up while my elderly mother is still living and still requires my assistance.

'Are you scared or anxious that work would bring back or worsen your illness?'

Yes. Of course.

'Can you look after yourself without help from others?'

I ticked Yes. Because my mother'is living with me. When she goes, that will be a different ball game.

'Do you get so upset by ordinary events that it results in disruptive behavioural problems?'

I ticked No. I'm always very well-contained.

'Do mental problems impair your ability to communicate with other people?'

I ticked No. So long as communication is at a very basic level, three pounds of potatoes and a bunch of carrots please, where no one expects me to be emotionally involved in any way, I can communicate just fine.

'Do you get irritated by things which would not have bothered you before becoming ill?'

I ticked No. I live a limited existence and the things that might irritate me are carefully excluded.

'Do you prefer to be alone for most of the day?'

I ticked No. This is actually a bit of a lie but if I said yes it might imply that I didn't want to be around my mother. In fact, I am alone for most of the day, up in my room, but I don't want to cut out my mother; she's all I have left.

'Are you too frightened to go out alone?'

I ticked No. I make myself walk the gauntlet every day.

There were other questions; they didn't seem to relate to me. I put the questionnaire in the envelope provided and sent it back.

An interview, an official interview. The first one in over thirty-five years. Still, it seemed that they were calling in everyone in order to make their million mark; there was no reason why I should not get an interview.

Lie down, the voice has told you
let gravity enfold you,
the world grows strained,
grey, colours drained.
As the word was said you faded.
To hide is senseless;
once you heard it you became parted,
from the growth of joy.
Had the words not crabbed
in your breast – the dancers we could
have joined – humours grabbed
from the gryphon's claws.
After the word, the long pause.

On the day of the interview, I dressed with care. I had no idea what sort of interview it was going to be. I had a bath and made sure all my clothes were clean. I didn't really know what to wear for an interview. The only winter coat I have is padded like an anorak. Should I wear my suit?

Over the preceding few days, I had become more and more agitated as the newspapers and radio continued to pump out the glad news of the large numbers of pensioners who were being redirected to the dole office. I was not very familiar with the centre of Hull and didn't know the best places to park. In the end, I decided to go by bus, something I hadn't done for years. That meant the anorak, shirt and tie, sweater and trousers. Clean and neat.

I caught the Hull bus. Many years ago, my sister came back for a holiday with two of her friends from Australia and at York station had asked a bus driver if his bus would take them to our town. He had indicated assent. 'Oh aye, its tha boos t'Ool.' The Australians were quite mystified, thus learning that in the rural heartland of England no one speaks intelligible English.

There were only three or four other people on the bus and I sat on the upper deck well away from everyone. More people got on as we went along. However, no one much came up to the upper deck. I felt, sitting there, that I looked pretty normal. Somebody was sitting further down in a similar anorak.

I turned up on time at the address. I sat in a chair. The doctor wrote notes. She asked the same sort of questions again as on the questionnaire, but then some other questions. She asked if I drank alcohol. I said yes, I liked to drink alcohol. That seemed normal to me. Everyone drinks alcohol. She asked me how many standard drinks I would have in a day. Standard drinks? What is a standard drink? On Sunday I would get a bottle of wine, sometimes another during the week. Screw tops are great; you don't have to drink the whole bottle on your own, you can leave half for the next day if you feel like it. When my younger sister comes, we can happily bang our way through a bottle together. How many drinks is that? None of our glasses match, apart from the Venetian ones in the china cabinet, thin spindly rose-coloured thimbles. Three, or four, or five of those? No, more probably. I said five tentatively. She wrote it down.

Then she wanted me to tell about the voices. This was slippery. I find it hard – no, impossible – to explain what goes on in my head. I learnt from way back at the beginning that if you give a doctor voices, her eyes will light up – aha, now we're onto something. There will be psychiatrists, treatment options, case notes, specialists, places to be sent, therapies to be tried, endless sitting on vinyl couches, endless waiting in dreary rooms. But if all you've got is a creaking sound, up in the attic where there are mice perhaps and an owl outside the window, the owl tracking the mice, the mice tracking the owl, a thick dusty fog – what do you tell a doctor? Better tell her you don't have any voices, because that will be easier for her. Better pretend to be normal.

Eventually, the interview was over and presumably she had the notes they wanted. I was drained; the effort was intense and constant. Everything they were wanting me to say was so deeply embarrassing, I couldn't bear it. Why couldn't they just leave me alone? Instead of holding up my failures like grey, soiled washing on the line.

When I finally got out, there was a breathless pounding in my chest and I also had an anxious premonition that the noise was coming back. It's not voices, it's like a whooshing sound in my head. The owl starting to flap.

I had intended to do a bit of shopping but I didn't feel sufficiently relaxed to do anything like that and made my way back to the bus station. There were quite a lot of people waiting, which added to my discomfort. I certainly didn't want to have to sit by anyone. When the bus came, I went up onto the upper deck and moved three-quarters of the way to the back, which I judged was probably the best place to sit if I wanted to fend off fellow passengers. I kept my gaze carefully out of the window so as to avoid eye contact with other people. No one looked normal any more. There are a lot of mad people on buses.

On the Buses

Fuck off he said
remembering fuck off each word
signifying some old humiliation
fuck off the rhythm harsh
fuck off the heat now so fierce
choking into flesh
fuck off fuck off each scar now burning
fuck off and old emotions churning
flooding whole remnants of wanting
now rewound fuck off fuck off
the pulse hammering
fuck off fuck off fuck off no truce of the mind
that fuels war no resigning
fuck off fuck off became all that was and is
in just one swearword fuck off fuck off fuck off scream
at each passenger fuck off fuck off fuck off
driven back into the seat
fuck off drawing this dart
into the soul pursuing what and where
fuck off fuck off blood was there
fuck off fuck off and drop by drop

it drips upon the fire
fuck off till dampened down
fuck off the flames go out.
Oh fuck
I think this is my stop.

'How did you go?' said my mother.
'It was all right,' I said.

But it wasn't. Someone in some office somewhere put on their black skull cap.

1 December 2006

Incapacity for work. I am writing to tell you the results of your Personal Capability Assessment, which looks at the way your illness or disability affects your everyday activities and, as a result, your ability to work.

To qualify for benefit or National Insurance credits, you need to score a minimum of 10 points in your Personal Capability Assessment.

As you scored 4 points we have decided that from 1 December 2006 you are not entitled to National Insurance credits.

If you are already getting income support you may no longer be entitled to Income Support because of your illness or disability. You will get a separate decision about this.

How we arrived at this decision. To work out your points, we used information from:
- the questionnaire you have filled in recently
- the report of the medical assessment you went to on 8 November 2006
- medical information from your own doctor.

My own doctor? What doctor? The doctor I saw in Hull was *your* doctor. Did I give them a name? Yes, sometime back in June. That would have been my mother's doctor, a GP who has never looked in my head and very rarely in any other part of me. My mother's doctor... is that why they asked me about alcohol?

Anyway, there it was: 4 out of 10. I can't even pass an exam in madness. Reminds me of my old report cards:

> The standard of Andrew's work is still far from satisfactory at this advanced stage of the course. Andrew is erratic and he cannot afford to persist in his casual approach. Andrew still has problems regarding this subject. He has worked quietly but only very limited progress has occurred, he must make a greater effort. Makes little response in class. Andrew's work is often of a mediocre standard and he seems to lack the interest or initiative to improve this situation. His casual attitude extends to his performance in the carrying out of school duties. He is always cheerful and polite.

I like the last bit. Even when I'm failing, I'm cheerful. Perhaps *because* I'm failing, I'm cheerful.

> failure compounds with the square
> misery mounts with the cube
> geometry delivers the food
> to nurture total despair

There was a following letter:

```
You are no longer entitled to Income Support, you are capable
of work from 1 December 2006, you must register with the
jobcentre, take this letter with you to the jobcentre, blah
blah blah if you disagree with this decision.
```

The freezing cold of those words. A judge pronouncing sentence of death presumably also has to write it down because it's not something the victim in the dock would hear properly first time; you can't take it in straight away. You think, this can't be happening to me. And if the prisoner isn't there and instead is, for instance, lying in a foetal position on his bed with a loud whooshing noise in his head, then definitely he'd need to have it in writing. You wouldn't take it on trust that such a decision had been made.

So there I had it, in writing. Twice.

I remember reading about two British drug traffickers tried in some

Asian country which has a habit of execution and they too were given sentence of death. They had put in an appeal and lost and their lawyer told the media that they were 'very disappointed'. It struck me how little prepared was any language to describe the passionless execution of a human being.

I always thought that there would be a reprieve for me. I thought someone would come to the house like the local manager did the last time. When the first letter came about the interview, my mother had tried to ring him but found that he had moved on. It seems that everyone had moved on and it wasn't the kind of service any more where people came to your house. Now they left you on your own. After thirty-five years of quietly sitting on the edge of the pool, I was being told to swim. I remember the flapping arms and the sickening taste of chlorine, the rubber tyre round my middle and the shouted instructions. I can't swim. I could never swim. My one attempt left me traumatised and withdrawn. I realised as the days went by and no one came that all I could do was quietly sink with as little fuss as possible. So I put the final letter away and tried to get on with it.

To start with, it was easy enough. Some time before, Mother had put a thousand pounds into my account in case, when she died, there were problems before the money could get sorted out and then I would have something to tide me over. Plus I had a small amount saved. To start with, I didn't cut down much at all. I kept expecting that intervention, that someone would come and it would all be put right again. But Christmas came and went and nothing appeared that could prop up the sky.

My mother's ninetieth birthday was to be celebrated in March. All of the family were coming. The tiler came to fix her new tiles in the bathroom. All the furniture had to be moved out of the sitting room so that a new carpet could be put in. Chaos reigned. These activities managed to hold it at bay, like a pain in the chest that you've got used to. My mother chose a red carpet for the sitting room; it bordered the aqua carpet of the corridor, the brown carpet of the kitchen and the purple carpet of the hall. My mother likes colour in her life.

My siblings arrived and were accommodated. My mother's cousins, her brother, my cousins and their children arrived and were spread out among hotels and accommodation places in the area. For about a week, there was a great deal of activity and I cooked many meals but was also taken out to eat at restaurants and pubs in the area. I got to drink convivial bottles of wine and pints of beer. Because I had put it out of my mind, the fact that I would probably not be seeing those family members again did not register. But now I have no regrets. I saw them for the last time in celebratory mood at my mother's birthday. I ate, drank and was merry, and so were they.

I get out of the car and go over and get a parking voucher. I don't want there to be any problem getting the car back. While I am putting it on the windscreen I suddenly realise that I need to write a note. Everybody leaves a note. I get back in the car while I think about this. I scrabble around and find an old envelope and a biro. I write down the first words that come into my head: 'I am sorry mother but I have put off doing this for too long.' She has kept me alive for the last thirty-five years, I hope she realises that. I try not to think that it was all a waste, because I don't want to die. If I did, I would have done it when the first letter arrived in December. I have left it to the very last minute when it is simply not possible to go on any longer.

Looking out of the car, I can see several people walking around on the cliffs. I'll wait until they all go; it's not a particularly nice evening so I can't imagine that will take long. Nearby, two young people are sitting with their arms around each other kissing. Maybe they think it's a romantic place, a public car park. If they went further off, there would be no one to look at them.

> The coupling time is the time around a point.
> Our moment is the time we rest from force
> and in the quiet centre of the storm anoint
> each other with a static charge and point our course
> and ease acceleration to a singularity.
> Let our spin be zero to dissolve in light

and make time shrink towards infinity.
Let us become a charge by our own energy
and super cooled from normal friction
magnetise our falling bodies to a fiction
of the hoped-for unified field theory.

The inside of the car is full of stuff. Plastic mackintoshes, walking sticks, umbrellas, road maps. I want to stop noticing small things, I want to see only air and sea and sky and great rushing clouds. I can't stay in the car. I get out and lock it and start to walk up the slope. Several people come down past me, their faces red with the wind. I keep my head down as they go past but once they're gone I can raise my head to look at the sky, the infinity of space for which I'm heading. In doing so, I miss my footing and suddenly fall heavily against the wooden guard rail, giving my head a sharp crack on a post.

It happens in the blink of an eye. All day I've been sleepwalking, keeping all feeling of reality at bay. I have tried to be a shell being moved about the shore by waves, completely inanimate. Thoughts filtered in unbidden: scraps of history, a mosaic of memories, small pleasures I've been saying goodbye to. But those parts of my being that fixed me in a certain place and at a certain time are automatic and don't detract at all from the role of waves bearing me inexorably along with the tide. And now I have arrived in this shifting grip, churned about but still on cue, believing that I could drift up and over the headland almost without volition. And I have come crashing down.

I lie there stunned for a few moments. I'm bewildered. This is not supposed to happen, this is not in the script. I'm suddenly very concerned that someone may have seen me, may be rushing even now to help me, oh horror. I immediately get up and stumble on as fast as possible even though I'm dripping blood on the path. I don't look to right or left; I clench my hands hard at my sides.

A short while later, I find a seat in a small enclosure out of the wind surrounded by shrubs, almost private. I sit down with my collar turned up so that no one passing will notice the blood on my head. I sit there listening like a hunted animal for footsteps. Time passes and no one comes.

I have lost the rhythm. Within the fraction of a second that I lay with my head on the rocky ground, I could see how it was going to be, the end. This has shaken me up. My head is full of scurrying thoughts, whereas before I was heading automaton-like towards a close. I had constructed this thick grey wall of polystyrene bricks, light enough to carry with me, wide enough to block out feelings, a fine defensive vehicle like having my own invisible tank. The sounds of life at the other side of this wall were muted and foggy like something happening in another room. The reason I had to get out of the car was really because the personal items that reminded me of my mother were allowing feelings to creep between the cracks, feelings of shame and despair at what I would leave. The note compounded it and I breathed a sigh of relief when I locked the car door, back in control again. That lasted such a short time. Falling over and hitting my head has ripped away my cushion and made a burst of loudness and reality when I least wanted it.

The problem is that my body won't always cooperate, especially of late. When I was young, I was quite good at cricket and not totally hopeless at soccer but I also could be quite ungainly at times. Once at school I got up from my desk to go to the blackboard, tripped over a metal strut and broke my leg. I got to spend several weeks at home, which was an excellent outcome and made up for the initial embarrassment of doing something so stupid. I was at boarding school by then, so being at home like that was a beautiful thing. The school is closed now; fortunately, no one sends their children to boarding schools any more unless they absolutely have to. Anyway, one school is pretty much as bad as another whether it's boarding or not. They all go on for far too long. All those years of study and exams, and then what? Then they let you out into the world of work and you find that what you're given to do you could have done at age twelve. Basic maths, a bit of mental arithmetic and spelling and grammar sufficient to turn out a decent two paragraph sentence reminding the recipient that as of the 25th ult they need to bring their arrears up to date. Working in an insurance company I realised that all of the things I learnt at secondary school were a complete waste of time.

Let me contemplate, for the purpose of soothing myself and calming down, what I will call the search for Newport Pagnell. Bernard Russell uses the first hundred pages of *Principia Mathematica* to prove the proposition that one plus one is two. All scientific philosophy for the last ninety years has been dedicated to proving this wrong. The error lies in the 'is', which must always be considered a shortcut through a more complex reality. All an equation can be is a description of a map of reality. 'Is' is the M1, while science is a search for Newport Pagnell. You have seen the name on the turn-off, and even stopped at the roadhouse, but can you prove the town exists without actually leaving your shortcut and moving through byways to find reality?

No one in an insurance office would be the slightest bit interested in a discussion along these lines. They're quite happy if you put one and one together and come up with two. And if you have the brains to find Newport Pagnell on a map and drive there by the most direct route, they would consider you to be managerial material.

I can only imagine that the need to force young people to stay at school so long springs from a number of motives.

Firstly, twelve-year-olds are difficult and unruly; even fourteen-year-olds can be unpleasant to deal with. By only taking new employees who have A levels, you are getting more mature people, hopefully. I point to Samuel Pepys, who took on a boy but then had to spend half his time beating him.

Secondly, there are too many kids coming through and this is a way of thinning out the way they hit the labour market.

Thirdly, children at posh schools have to learn a lot more in order to go out and take up the burden of empire. Apparently, in order to control the teeming millions of India, you had to be able to conjugate Virgil and have at least a smattering of Greek. So when compulsory schooling came in, this became the desired level of attainment and it takes a long time to learn Latin. I know, I've tried it. Unfortunately for all this effort, most office jobs do not require you to be able to translate 'These things having been done, Caesar crossed the Rubicon'. Nor for that matter do you need to know anything about the Corn Laws, the geology of the Urals, Poisson's ratio of material in wave theory, or 'John Lennon is it poetry, discuss'. You just need to know how to stay awake, get through the day and not spend all your money on beer.

> Rhythm builds the bank
> becoming both wave and particle
> till mass reaches a point that's critical.
> All conflicts that rhythm unites
> function as a chrism of the harmonic
> or spasm of the plastic art
> that transforms all details on the chart.

I chose to do science at school and my mother blames this for all my present problems. She thinks I should have done English literature. But what good does literature do? At least with science, if I had been any good at it, I would have had a hope of passing my days in unsociable laboratories unremarked among all the other odd sorts. But I wasn't any good at it. Pity, because I also truly believed once that I could do some good in the world. As I got older, I stopped believing that. When you get it into your head that everyone is going to die, saving the world seems a nonsense.

I don't want to think about my school. I don't want to think about my ghastly first and only job in that insurance company. I don't want to blame anyone. Or if I do blame someone, then let it be Labour Party politicians who have let down the most vulnerable in the name of populism. But I don't blame my parents or my family, or my teachers, not my ex-boss, no one. I arrived here with my present peculiarities entirely under my own steam.

All tests show that clinical depressives
see the world more clearly than the sane.
Sanity is a delusive state
that needs constant repair. You must gain
a stereotype to scaffold round your soul
because problems you must solve cause stress
and too much stress leads to depression.
If you choose a pack façade to think and dress
and act, you will lose most of your tension.
But always be aware that your reality is unreal
so that in any crisis you can switch
to logic instead of the rail tracks of what you feel.
But logic can only offer limited choice
and on a corridor leading to two doors
to choose you must listen to your inner voice.
Psychiatry always fails to see the cause,
'truth' is only the cutout it is based upon.
Ask the suicide before he tops himself
if you really want to know what's going on.

    I think I've stopped bleeding. The collar of my shirt now feels dry and the side of my head, although it still smarts, is no longer radiating pain. I feel terrible. I had been aiming at what I would call an easy transition. A stroll slowly up the hill when everyone else had gone home, the luxury of contemplation, an unhurried exit. But now I'm a complete mental mess. When I tripped, I spoilt the pattern and now I don't know what to do. It enters my head that I could go back, call in at a doctor and get stitches, pretend to my mother that I did it in the garden and drove off to... No. It's too late, far too late. She'll be home by now. How long before she realises I'm not in my room? How long before she notices the car is gone? Once she notices the car, she'll know straight away, nothing I say will unconvince her, she'll dig and delve, she'll get to the truth of the matter. I can't go back, because I couldn't bear that – to be a case again that has to be solved. No, nothing has changed and the hopelessness of my situation again strikes me and I feel bitterness swell like a taste in my mouth.

If I sit thinking about it long enough, maybe I can re-enter my previous state. Otherwise the terror will destroy me and I won't be able to function. Then it will be back to those awful awful National Health places. I must succeed this time.

I see that the couple have moved round to a lawn below me where they're becoming a lot more intimate. It's almost as if they knew I was here and are making out in front of me on purpose. In the west, the sun is setting and on the grass are two kids fucking. Fucking, it's an ugly word.

> It is not a real word
> it is a 16th century euphemism
> which meant to beat.
> You could have said you accessed
> bonked or banged her
> chuffed or dorked her
> entered or gunned her
> gentled or had her
> invaded or jabbed her
> knobbed or lanced her
> mounted or picked her
> overthrew or pinned her
> quimmed or rammed her
> saddled or tupped her
> up ended or valved her
> whammed or explored
> or zonked her. So why choose
> the one word she will recognise,
> that will offend her?
> Did you, as you pushed and shoved,
> choose it to show she was hated
> and not loved?

Maybe if it doesn't work out, one of them will come and jump off too. But not today. They seem rather uninhibited flamboyant types, not at all the kind of people I would like to jump in tandem with. I'm waiting for everyone to go so I can guarantee maximum privacy. When the coast is clear. That's a funny saying. I wonder where that came from. Probably from smuggling. There was a lot of smuggling around here. Maybe that's what I should have done with my life. If I'd saved up and bought a boat, I could have gone over to France and brought back a few crates of nice Bordeaux, not the Australian varietals but something complex and demanding. I could have come back in the dark and put into one of these little coves, just like it's always been done. If the coast was clear.

As I said before, I used to dream of saving the world. But as I got older and more mortal, my only dream was to be rich. Do people get rich smuggling wine? I don't think so, otherwise you'd hear about it in the paper, people getting caught. You don't see people being executed in Thai jails for carrying illicit South African Cabernet.

So much for materialism. It never got me anywhere and it never will. Rich or poor, we all come at last to the same place.

> By fierce struggle I have left the fertile plains
> scorned the prosperous foothills
> ignored the forested slopes
> arrived at the glacier where purity lies.
> The ice white,
> the rocks grey,
> scoured clear,
> melt water carries the crushed residue to gleaming reefs
> and I am cleansed of the messiness of life.

Time has passed. I've hardly been aware of it. The moon is coming out. I get up to go. I feel resigned now and hopefully that will be enough. I have a heavy heart and my cheeks are wet; there must be dew about. The young lovers have gone. Maybe they heard me – that would be embarrassing. Much more embarrassing than having sex where someone can see you. Everything is relative. The blow on the head nearly undid me. In that fleeting fraction of a second, I saw, as if looking down from above, my inanimate body lying on the rocks, crime scene tape up here on the cliff, men from the lifeboat coming ashore and grappling to get me off, everything to the putter-putter sound of a helicopter's rotating blades. This was a very fast newsreel to the accompanying abattoir smell of blood and death.

Anyway, this is fantasy. Everything in the moonlight is distorted and surreal, passing by as if on a snowy night. I must walk carefully. I don't want to come a cropper again. The pain breaks in in a way I didn't expect.

> The smoking chimney hung without context
> a magician's trick floating unsupported
> over a brick box where flickerings reflected
> on lower window panes and porches.
> As I came closer I saw the old snowed eaves
> part from the pale grey sky to show the sleeve
> of nature's sleight. The black hedge under white
> and the sound of each booted step spoke
> of the sleeping cold, or did the sharp bite
> mean these boots now leak. I hawk
> the phlegm in my throat afraid to spit
> for if the sticky snot string stuck
> to my anorak I would have to take
> my hands out of pockets to clear it
> from nostrils burdened with cold. Was it snowing
> or was it about to? The flat light
> did not say. But the random sting
> on the face seemed too cold for snow.
> Colour bled from the scene until white and black
> were the only shade
> and I had many miles to go
> to a final hearth with no fire laid.

I'm getting off the authorised paths and going over to the northern side, where there's a big bird sanctuary. I came here years and years ago with my uncle before it was so regulated. You could wander anywhere and fall off if you felt like it – no one took any responsibility for you then. Now there are signs everywhere, barricades, warnings. As if the population of North England is in danger of following the coastline into the sea.

Puffins. That's what my uncle came for with his fellow Ramblers. They would get out their binoculars and look for them. They weren't twitchers, just elderly naturalists from Rotherham. They're sweet birds, puffins, like jaunty children – I also like to think they're harmless. Birds are pretty harmless as a rule. But a scientist fell down a cliff, in Antarctica I think; my Australian sister was telling me about it. He was still alive but before they could get him out he was pecked at by birds. Maybe they were skuas – with a name like that...

This sister tells me things which are not a great advertisement for the Australian Tourist Board, in terms of horrible things happening to people out in the open air. For instance, she told me that more people die through lightning strikes on golf courses in Australia than are taken by sharks. This is medium-good news for those swimming in the sea but not such good news for those who enjoy golf. I used to enjoy golf, when I had someone to play with. It's a solitary game where you go round the course with one or two other people hitting a ball, and then at the end you add up your scorecard and someone has won. If I'd kept up the golf, perhaps I wouldn't be so unfit. Anyway, to get back to the scientist, he died sometime later, but I'm not sure whether it was the birds' peck or the fall that eventually did for him.

The trick is to get the height. Twenty feet isn't necessarily enough. Fifty feet, you'd be much more sure. But a glorious hundred-metre freestyle, you can't fail, and a bird's peck is neither here nor there.

> the pine clings to the mountain
> the iron waits in the earth
> sky hangs down a grey curtain
> around the hole in the turf
>
> cut and plank the pine
> mine and shape the nails
> blot with black sunshine
> where the dead grass pales

> the final gasping lumber
> to try for one more moment
> but breath on fading embers
> prolongs again the torment

It's a heavy climb up but I know I'll make it now. My heart is pounding, my sobs burst out again and a few late birds, hung on dipping wires by an invisible puppeteer, make thin sad sounds. Soon there will be nothing to the north of me except Arctic wonderland. My sobs open out into a howl – Help me, Help me – as I come up onto the brow, into the full force of the great wind. Now the gale is trying to fight me back, screaming and whipping my hair, grasping wildly at my clothes. I'm pushed to my knees like a man praying, but I'm not praying because there's no one to pray to.

I hoped I could do this calmly or at least clinically but I realise now there's no way out except in a storm of braying tears. I stand up. I will not be denied, because there is nowhere else for me. I push through the coward's barrier that holds us all back and I arrive at last at my pure house of ice, where the crystals tinkle faintly in the plume of frost.

This book is dedicated to the brave men of the Bridlington Lifeboat Service who recovered the body of Andrew Mackirdy in challenging conditions at considerable risk to their own lives.

www.ingramcontent.com/pod-product-compliance
Lightning Source LLC
Chambersburg PA
CBHW030914080526
44589CB00010B/303